UNRAVELING THE ASSESSMENT INDUSTRIAL COMPLEX

D0911582

This book offers a comprehensive critique of how the assessment industry and standardized testing adversely impact students, teachers, and society. The authors present the case that the interconnected developments of the testing industry and the Assessment Industrial Complex (AIC) have effectively anchored American schooling to testing. Using an antiracist lens, the authors deconstruct the AIC, exposing the neoliberal agenda of education reformers and how proponents utilize the rhetoric of testing, and the data extracted from them, to normalize the reliance on AIC systems. This critique further exposes education reformers' ideological agenda, their hypocrisy, and how they grossly profit from the AIC at the expense of society's marginalized and most vulnerable students. The COVID-19 pandemic, society's racial unrest, and anti-testing movements have aligned to underscore the need to examine systemic oppression and the impact it has on society through our education system. This text exposes how standardized testing perpetuates these injustices and provides the opportunity to disrupt the systems they rely upon and bolster the societal resistance that is needed.

Michelle Tenam-Zemach, EdD, is a Professor of Curriculum and Instruction at Nova Southeastern University. Michelle's areas of scholarly interest include curriculum theory, assessment, pedagogy, and teacher and faculty personal and professional development. She is committed to promoting the principles of equity, social justice, access, and opportunity in the realm of education and beyond. When she is not busy working, Michelle focuses on cycling, yoga, reading, cooking, and spending time with her family.

Daniel R. Conn, EdD, is an Associate Professor of Teacher Education at Minot University. Daniel's scholarly interests include curriculum, social justice aesthetics in education, and ecological education. Daniel is a founding member of a non-profit, dreamBIG Green Schools, which aims to engage local communities in dialogue and action related to climate change. When he is not teaching and researching, Daniel enjoys running, swimming, biking, hiking, camping, coaching, and spending time with his family—Linda, Virginia, Miles, and many pets.

Paul T. Parkison, EdD, is a Professor and Chair of the Department of Teaching, Learning, and Curriculum at the University of North Florida. His most recent scholarship has appeared in *The Education Forum, Critical Education, Journal of Curriculum Theorizing,* and *Curriculum and Teaching Dialogue.*

UNRAVELING THE ASSESSMENT INDUSTRIAL COMPLEX

Understanding How Testing Perpetuates Inequity and Injustice in America

Michelle Tenam-Zemach, Daniel R. Conn, and Paul T. Parkison

Routledge
Taylor & Francis Group

NEW YORK AND LONDON

First published 2021
by Routledge
52 Vanderbilt Avenue, New York, NY 10017

and by Routledge
2 Park Square, Milton Park, Abingdon, Oxon, OX14 4RN

Routledge is an imprint of the Taylor & Francis Group, an informa business

© 2021 Taylor & Francis

The right of Michelle Tenam-Zemach, Daniel R. Conn, and Paul T. Parkison to be identified as the authors of the material has been asserted in accordance with sections 77 and 78 of the Copyright, Designs and Patents Act 1988.

Library of Congress Cataloging-in-Publication Data
Names: Tenam-Zemach, Michelle, editor. | Conn, Daniel R., editor. | Parkison, Paul T., editor.
Title: Unraveling the assessment industrial complex : how testing perpetuates inequity and injustice in America / edited by Michelle Tenam-Zemach, Daniel R. Conn, Paul T. Parkison.
Description: New York, NY : Routledge, 2021. | Includes bibliographical references and index.
Identifiers: LCCN 2020044470 (print) | LCCN 2020044471 (ebook) | ISBN 9780367426453 (hardback) | ISBN 9780367407872 (paperback) | ISBN 9780367854065 (ebook)
Subjects: LCSH: Educational tests and measurements--Social aspects--United States. | Capitalism and education--United States. | Educational equalization--United States. | Neoliberalism--United States.
Classification: LCC LB3051 .U587 2021 (print) | LCC LB3051 (ebook) | DDC 371.260973--dc23
LC record available at https://lccn.loc.gov/2020044470
LC ebook record available at https://lccn.loc.gov/2020044471

ISBN: 978-0-367-42645-3 (hbk)
ISBN: 978-0-367-40787-2 (pbk)
ISBN: 978-0-367-85406-5 (ebk)

Typeset in Bembo
by MPS Limited, Dehradun

We dedicate this book to all the students in this country who should no longer be subjected to the oppressive will and actions of adults. Now more than ever, our children need the guidance, love, and compassion of all adults; they need us to do the right thing for our environment, our schools, and our society.

CONTENTS

ACKNOWLEDGMENTS

Throughout the development of this book, we were eternally grateful for all the support we received from our colleagues, family, and friends. While each deserves a special thanks, we particularly would like to acknowledge several people who took their time to guide our work, critique its contents, and share in our frustrations with the AIC. Dr. David Stovall, who provided the foreword, served as a mentor and guide; we thank him for his contributions, time, and attention to this book. We cannot describe our gratitude to Dr. Derek Gottlieb. His honest critique helped us to maintain a level of integrity and balance we may not have achieved otherwise, and his vision of and commitment to this book, from its inception to its completion, was a critical component of its development. As educators committed to a more just education system and world, we would also like to thank Dr. Bruce Uhrmacher for keeping us honest and brave. His comments on our words and ideas helped us to question our thinking and our beliefs; we are all better humans as a result. We also would like to thank Drs. William White, Joseph Flynn, and David Escobar for reviewing our initial book proposal and supporting our work. We offer endless thanks to Dr. Catharine Mattox, whose love of all things done RIGHT facilitated the completion of the final manuscript. Additionally, we would be remiss if we did not give special thanks to two extraordinary young people: Virginia Conn, whose creativity and passion infused beauty into this text, and Joel Zemach, who offered critique and insight that at times was much needed. Finally, we would each like to thank our spouses and children for their love, patience, and support throughout the development of this project.

FOREWORD: BECAUSE WE KNOW THERE IS NO EXCUSE FOR DOING NOTHING

David Omotoso Stovall PhD

In his classic text *The Mismeasure of Man*, Stephen Jay Gould dared to challenge the scientific community by stating that the potential of human beings could never be measured by a singular set of numbers resulting from a battery of tests. Tukufu Zuberi, in taking Gould's points further in his book *Thicker Than Blood*, connects the fallacy of biological race to White supremacist machinations of Western Europe, arguing for the intellectual superiority of those classified as White over the populations of the vast majority of the globe. His careful analysis reveals the commitment of mainstream science to White supremacy in the form of constructed trials (tests) created to determine intellect as emblematic of a world that continues to justify gratuitous punishment on the lives of Black and Brown people in perpetuity.

I am reminded of Zuberi and Gould's willingness to unearth the lie placed forward by members of the academic and scientific communities in the following pages of this necessary and thought-provoking book. In the intimately connected pandemics of COVID-19, White supremacy, and capitalism, naming the absurdity of standardized testing is of critical importance as K–12 school districts and institutions of higher education recognize the uselessness of tests to predict or determine life outcomes or competency in a particular content area. As the lies continue to be unearthed by those committed to interrupting what is referenced as the Assessment Industrial Complex (AIC), the connection to economic schemes aimed at prioritizing the needs of the wealthy through private control of public goods (neoliberalism) looms large. The big business of testing has morphed into multi-million-dollar long-term contracts with public education districts to provide testing to further sort and regulate Black and Brown populations that have historically had fewer resources. I am clear that testing makes way for the neoliberal trope of the centrality of "individual responsibility" that results in the blame of students for not having what they need when they need it (equity). Given this reality, I also understand this book as making a tangible connection to the realization that the current socio-political moment of resistance to state-sanctioned violence in the form of police brutality, inadequate K–20 education, housing insecurity, disparities in health care, food security, and unemployment, like the resistance to high-stakes testing, is long overdue.

The provocation of assessment as an "industrial complex" is appreciated as it directly confronts the transformation of assessment from sorting mechanism to instrument of late stage capitalism (business). Similar to the Prison Industrial Complex (PIC), as the overlapping interests of government and industry to use the technologies of policing and imprisonment to solve social, political, and economic problems, the AIC operates in like fashion. As a process centered in the convergence of the interests of political, social, and economic entities, one of the goals of the AIC is to ensure the permanent indenture of K–20 schooling systems. "Control" is too simple a construct to describe the grip of the AIC on school systems. Indenture speaks to a perpetual debt until released from the grips of tyranny. Given the breadth and depth of the AIC, it has become a totalizing power in K–20 education, akin to the grip that capitalism and White supremacy have on the planet.

To some, the current moment in K–20 education at first glance may appear to be insurmountable. However, I am less discouraged by the current moment and find myself encouraged by this book and its unapologetic stance to name and resist the AIC. Just as opponents of the PIC have called for its abolition, I understand the contents of this book to operate in similar fashion. Because this account is clear as to how the machinations of industry have incorporated the AIC to further extract the labor of the exploited and disenfranchised in schools (in the form of test prep, test taking, proctoring, etc.), we should also consider its abolition. If we know there is little reliability or validity in testing to assess the capacity of our students to face insurmountable odds, live in eternal precarity, or face White supremacy head-on, sometimes facing imminent death, then we have no choice but to question the validity and viability of the AIC. The organization Critical Resistance reminds us that abolition is a long-term political vision seeking to shrink the institutions that harm us into non-existence. We should be giving the same thought and action to high-stakes testing, college admissions that are weighted by standardized test scores, and early childhood testing. Our lives have become dreadfully intimate with the AIC—many of us have been victimized by it for far too long. If our lives as educators are committed to the end of suffering (including our own) at the hands of school districts and ineffective mandated curricula, we have no choice but to consider the work of abolishing a system (the AIC) that does not do right by us. I cannot see another group of third graders given cookies with nothing to drink to sit and suffer while they take a test. I will not watch another group of high schoolers panicked to no end because they feel as if their entire lives depend on an SAT or ACT score. Not one more school needs to be placed on probation because they did not hit the arbitrary "meets or exceeds" set by its respective state or district. Young people, parents, family members, and teachers are fed up. Trying to reform a tragic system rooted in subjugation and repression is futile. If there is ever a moment to put abolition of the AIC in our sights, the time is now.

In closing, I remain humbled by the fact that Michelle Tenam-Zemach, Daniel Conn, and Paul Parkison have allowed me to provide some opening remarks for an exceedingly important and urgent manuscript. Collectively they have made the decision to name the evil of the high-stakes, standardized, eugenic, White-supremacist testing industry in its totality. In a daring move to tell a tragic, but necessary, truth, I understand their work to be in solidarity with the scores of people who are currently in the streets on every continent demanding justice for the fallen and exploited. Many of these people who are making these challenges to the system are students, K–12 teachers, administrators, college professors, and researchers who are or have been deeply traumatized by the tentacles of the AIC. I am thankful for their push to demand that suffering at the hands of White supremacy in the form of testing must end. This book stands as testament that their efforts are not in vain. At the same time, I am clear that the work ahead will continue to be difficult but remains to be of great consequence. Because we cannot rest on the laurels of knowing these things to be true, the imperative of moving from thought to action remains clear. Once you read this book, I hope that you do not let it rest in your brain as solely provocative text. Instead, I hope it moves you to work with others toward the abolition of the AIC. What we've known for so long cannot continue to ravage our communities and the people we say we love. We have been challenged to do something other than talk about the intentional damage of the AIC in secrecy. The secret is out. At this point, you will either join the resistance or choose to perish with an enemy that continues to profit from your suffering. In the end, I think the aforementioned options leave you with a pretty simple choice.

INTRODUCTION

The Upside Down

Netflix currently has a popular original series called "Stranger Things." In the show, there is an alternate dimension referred to as "The Upside Down" (The Upside Down, n.d.), a world that is parallel to the human world. Although The Upside Down is a fictionalized rendering of a paranormal world experienced by several of the characters in the show, quite often, the ethereal nature of this strange world seems to resemble what we, the authors of this text, are experiencing today in education and beyond. When we began crafting this book (much before the COVID-19 pandemic), none of us could have imagined a time where everything we experienced in our lives would reflect a strange and surreal pattern of existence. Suddenly, and seemingly out of nowhere, we were all asked, then mandated, to just stop what we were doing, how we were living, and how we conceived of our everyday reality. We were also expected to reinvent our daily routines and lives immediately. For many of us who work remotely part or full time, such changes were perhaps less devastating in terms of our everyday work experiences, but for the vast majority of Americans and beyond, this was something completely unimaginable. Add the forced confinement with our children and separation from our elders, and most people seem confounded with how to coexist (or live without) people they generally see before 8 am and after 5 pm (of course, this varies across individuals and families).

More interesting is the reaction of our public institutions. In the case of schools, they were summarily closed, at first for a few weeks, and inevitably, as reality loomed its dreary head, for the remainder of the school year. Again, for college and high school students and faculty already learning and teaching online, this may not have presented an enormous struggle. Still, for the vast majority of Americans, this was nothing short of catastrophic. Suddenly, parents are their children's teachers, and teachers, many of whom have children to care for, had to expeditiously contrive methods for shifting their face-to-face instruction and content online with little if any professional development or time to prepare.

Anecdotes abound of parents struggling to balance the academic, emotional, and social needs of their children while working from home. Others, who swiftly became unemployed, shared accounts of their concerns with not being able to feed or care for their children, much less facilitate the demands of their children's teachers and schools. For an interesting analysis of the anger and frustration one Israeli mother experienced, watch her translated video (Kenigsberg Levi, 2020). Another mother posted a YouTube video, which, as of this publication, has had over 1.7 million views. In this funny yet all too realistic video, the mother states, "Let us pray. Father God, I am a child of God. What I am not, is a homeschool teacher. God, I'm at home, but Lord, ain't no teaching going on around here…" (Shropshire, 2020, 01:46). Clearly, this parent understands her circumstances, but what she may fail to understand is how her perspective is shaped, in part, by the current rhetoric of education reform. She states, "Lord God, the spirit of Common Core has attacked our household, and right now, the only thing we have in common is frustration and no answer to the math problem, Lord God." In a different YouTube offering called Some Good News, John Krasinski (2020, 05:47), a celebrity actor, discusses the challenges of homeschooling. In a segment called "Nice Job Parents," he points out that "in speaking from experience, after homeschooling for only two weeks, I am damned near at the end of my rope, and I am only doing six-year-old math. For those of you with kids over six [here, he raises a glass of wine and states] Good Luck!" Humor aside, parents seem to struggle with the understanding that educating their children matters, but that, for many, they are ill-equipped to handle the expectations that have been forced upon them in this crisis. They do seem to acknowledge, though, that these challenges are common for teachers in contemporary schooling (Long, 2020).

One must wonder, why parents are being asked to bear the burden of educating their children under such stressful and unique circumstances? Our country has limitless creative potential and deep respect for community, particularly in the time of a crisis. (Think back to the country's call for unification after the terrorist attacks of 9/11.) Couldn't we do more than concern ourselves with ensuring that our students do not "fall behind" or fear they won't be able to "catch up." "Falling behind" and "catching up" to what? Aren't all students in the same situations? These ideas only make sense within a view of schooling that is defined by testing and test scores. Constructs such as these are designed to keep parents and their children engaged in an oppressive perspective of what it means to educate kids in the US today. But as Westheimer (2020) cautions us, "We've spent the last 25 years over-scheduling kids, over-testing kids, putting undue pressure on them to achieve more and more and play less and less. The result? Several generations of children and young adults who are stressed-out, medicated, alienated, and depressed" (paragraph 2). Westheimer also reminds us of what can be gained "for those of us lucky enough to be at home and not in hospitals or driving buses…" (paragraph 3). Our current reality is a unique opportunity for parents to engage with their children, examine their priorities, understand their children's needs, and challenge a system that is not working for so many, and working for too few. But how can we attempt to understand who our children are and reinvent our relationships with them, when too many parents are fretting over how they will feed themselves and their children?

Deb Perelman, in her July 2, 2020, *The New York Times* article "In the CoVid-19 Economy, You Can Have a Kid or a Job. You Can't Have Both" expresses the frustration and anxiety many parents are feeling. COVID-19 has highlighted and brought to the attention of an increasing number of people the disparity of support that exists for students in schools. Perhaps the most wide-reaching change brought about by the COVID-19 pandemic is the nation-wide school closures, which are forcing millions of American parents to homeschool their children while teachers attempt to engage them in online learning. Even in schools where administrators are bringing classes online, teachers are facing immense barriers to students' active participation; a lot of responsibility has fallen on the parents to ensure the continued education of their children. Many parents are struggling to juggle working from home, running a household, and possibly taking care of sick family members, all while teaching their children math, English, science, and history. As with every other aspect of society during the pandemic, school closures are reproducing and often intensifying structural inequalities along racial and socioeconomic lines. Low-income parents and parents of color are more likely to be "essential workers" who cannot stay home with their children. Furthermore, they may not have the equipment or internet access necessary for their children to participate in schools' remote programs. Wealthy parents, contrarily, have the resources in either time or treasure or both to support their children's education to a far greater extent than those living on the margins. It is not a matter of interest or concern; it is a matter of time and energy.

Time for a Power Grab

We live, to be blunt, in a society with vast inequality. And it is this inequality that perpetuates ongoing power grabs by large corporations seeking to profit from tragedy. For example, consider a recent special report published by ASCD entitled "A New Reality: Getting Remote Learning Right" (ASCD, 2020). The stated intent is to propose guidance to schools and teachers on how to successfully and efficaciously address this "crisis." What is particularly interesting about this report is Kognito, a health simulation company, sponsored it. Embedded in its pages are advertisements for Kognito: "Meet your educators (any)where they are" (p. 1) and, "Kognito's interactive simulations are designed to empower educators to support the social and emotional health of students" (p. 15). This is one example of what we extensively discuss in this book: The instrumentalization of education via assessments and how market-driven forces are usurping power to engender their solutions as vital to solving educational "problems." And as we also demonstrate throughout this text, various entities manufacture "problems" with a specific agenda to undermine public education to profit from it. The instrumentalization of our schools and education system (and eventually our thinking) is made up of small, incremental moves and tactics, a ratcheting up of initiatives and programs that introduce new possibilities and innovations, all framed as essential reforms of failing institutions. Policies and practices that previously seemed unthinkable, with time, become common sense and the obvious of policy, as "what works" and as "best practice;" such reforms become embedded in a "necessarian logic," most commonly relating to the necessities of competitiveness. Once established, these reforms and policies make further moves thinkable and doable, and ultimately make them obvious and indeed necessary. The assemblages that are solidified as instruments of "competitive necessity" enframe and entrap our schools and classrooms and our ability to respond to the unique and unforeseen. Decentering this enframing (Deleuze & Guattari, 1987) has the potential to open a new space for creative thinking and responsiveness. But by framing "shelter-in-place" or "stay-at-home" orders as problems that need to be solved by edtech and other companies, we forgo an opportunity as a nation to re-envision the role of education, teaching, and learning in society. Perhaps this is a moment for change, for rethinking what we value as a society, as educators, as parents. Perhaps this is a once-in-a-lifetime opportunity to redefine the purpose and meaning of educating our children.

Enframing and the Assessment Industrial Complex

We claim that contemporary education assessment, and standardized assessment specifically, has become the dominant way of being and doing: Assessment anchors education to a specific mode of being a teacher, a student, and even a parent. Rather than being facilitators of learning and learners, teachers and students are involved in test preparation. Standardized assessment increasingly mediates, or, more precisely, filters out, a vast array of educational endeavors. In the data-driven and high-stakes accountability schooling system, testing has become the way we teach, the way we learn, the way we determine effectiveness, and so forth. It has become subsumed into every aspect of our human and educational institutions. This has led testing of all forms to become the raison d'etre of education, and several scholars have referred to testing as an industrial complex in its own right (Roberts, 2015). Roberts argues, "the Testing Industrial complex [TIC] is a system in which high-stakes standardized testing fuels neoliberal education reforms. The 'reforms' create a system in which curriculum, students, and teachers become currencies traded for corporate profit" (p. 153). Conn and Tenam-Zemach (2019) build on similar concepts, stating that "The Assessment Industrial Complex is an amalgam of corporate interests and neoliberal and neoconservative education reformers.... We coined the phrase 'Assessment Industrial Complex' [AIC] to underscore the vast array of stakeholders involved who ultimately profit from this system of assessment and accountability" (p. 123). Whether it is called the TIC or AIC, or some other acronym, testing causes the essential human elements of the classroom, teacher–student and student–student relationships, joy, exploration, and engagement to not make their way through the testing sieve. Standardized assessments and, through them, the AIC exert control over our education policy; our schools; our classrooms; our curriculum; our instruction; our classroom-based relationships; our professional identities as teachers, professors, and much more within education. Who our students are is reduced to a test score (Knoester & Parkison, 2017; Parkison, 2009), often associated more with a student ID number than a name.

The AIC enframes our continual pursuit of impact and effectiveness. As teachers, schools, and communities, we "delegate" to standardized assessment creators, the AIC, the most intimate details of our educational pursuits, and we conveniently forget and lose track of the source of these interventions. Under the surface of our work within education, an increasingly complex system of data generation, gathering, and analysis is evolving with its own emergent performative outcomes—a performativity in which learning is but a faint echo, silently shaping our present and future possibilities for becoming diverse individuals with diverse interests, passions, and aspirations. These become homogenized by a standardized schooling experience. In the process of this instrumental standardization, the performativity of the AIC institutionalizes racist, sexist, and classist structures through the symbolic violence of data and accountability.

What has become exposed within the AIC world is how teachers, schools, and communities continuously perform their educational productivity—it is as much display as production. There are assumptions, collective taken-for-granted beliefs, about our productivity when we take a test. Time devoted to assessment has become accepted as productive work time in educational settings. When we consider the human elements, the relationships inherent to schooling, we eliminate that illusion. Grounded in the three "technologies" of market, management, and performance, instrumentalism inconspicuously, but harmfully, changed the subjective experience of education at all levels (Heidegger, 1977). The power of standardization in service delivery gives rise to change in education as part of a slow ossification. Data-driven management is altering social connections and power relations to less democratic and caring forms, and performativity and accountability agendas are radically undermining the professionalism of administrators and teachers in the hunt for measures, targets, benchmarks, tests, tables, audits, and uniform/homogeneous policies (best if equally adopted by peer institutions) to feed the system in the name of improvement.

As teachers and students, we are exposed and surveilled in the AIC world through data collection and assessment. The AIC world is a panoptical scene. In the panoptical scene, the appearance of certain "elements"—computer test banks, formative data walls, Lexile scores, achievement gaps, falling behind, and catching up—are observational data brought into being and sustained through performance and accountability, which is to say power's attentions. They are in that sense the coerced actualizations of virtual potential in which an assemblage of material elements—inter/intra-organization communication, recognition and full-presence, backgrounds, relationships, and normalized attention—are entangled and somehow coordinated. Proof of this diagnosis is in its observable trace: Parents' struggle with understanding that educating their children matters, but that the expectations that have been forced upon them in this pandemic crisis do not align to their instincts as parents and expectations for their children. Schooling's enfolding into the habits and demeanor of the teachers and students, and henceforth of the "subjectivity" they display and articulate, and in the persuasiveness of the argument that posits this analysis as a convincing probability feels incongruous.

Standardized assessments seem to configure and circumscribe us and our educational lives in more or less significant ways. They define what is relevant and what is not, what needs attending to and what does not — legitimating particular ways of learning while simultaneously delegitimizing (or rendering more or less obscure) equally valid alternatives. As students routinely ask, "Is this going to be on the test?" and see relevance as determined by the ability to be credentialed, teachers feel the impact of this circumscription. Students fully realize this restriction of their potential education to testing and credentialing as a violent assault on their lives and futures. Where this becomes evident is in the intense focus on career as students enter high school and is the point behind a proliferating breed of career-interest inventories, self-assessments, and aptitude tests that school districts are using to help steer students to a future vocation. This emphasis is paralleled by a dramatic increase in high school (Mulvenon, Stegman, & Ritter, 2005) and college students' stress and anxiety.

In and through these assessment practices developed and sold to schools by the AIC, an assessment-driven "technological unconscious" is emerging, which sustains a symbolically powerful system. It is in and through these standardized assessment landscapes where many of the ontological questions of our future within education are being determined (even if this determination is contingent and emergent). As such, this introduction renders visible some of the contours of the phenomenon of assessment. In doing this, it will, however, not only focus on standardized testing, important as this may be, but it also will suggest a broader understanding of the phenomenon of assessment as an enframing construct within education. It may also render visible some of the concerns and contradictions in contemporary discourse concerning schooling as anchored by the AIC.

We present a preliminary sketch in three steps. First, we provide an outline sketch of some of the central notions of the phenomenon of assessment. Second, we offer a brief discussion of the testing industry and extension of agency from standards to assessment, to curriculum, and finally to accountability systems. Third, we take a small detour to look at accountability systems in the context of teaching and learning practices to reveal how multiple and intersecting AIC systems overlap with many unexpected performative outcomes. Most important in this detour is the more general question of the curriculum (and by implication its opposite, the scripted lesson) in all assessment-driven enactments of learning and teaching. The AIC's system of high-stakes testing, accountability, and league tables circumscribes the daily lives of students. Students' educational experience is one of competition and scorekeeping. Learning, wondering, exploring, and relating are pushed to the margins of their experience.

Central Notions of the Phenomenon of Assessment

When referring to the notion of *assessment*, we have in mind a vast array of normatively governed material enactments such as standardized tests, formative assessment software, data analysis, and usage protocols; accountability regimes; content standards alignment and mapping strategies; instructional planning and fidelity; high-leverage instructional strategies; best practices; classroom management protocols; instructional scripts; educational software; and so forth. Some of these assessments are seemingly rigid/explicit and may be the outcome of more or less explicit design intentions and decisions. Others are more malleable/implicit and emerge as a more or less collateral outcome of ongoing socio-material ordering practices. We suggest that within the current schooling regime, assessments are. norm- or rule-governed material enactments accepted (or taken for granted) as the necessary conditions for teachers to teach what students are supposed to learn.

Two aspects of this demarcation of schooling as assessment-driven and controlled by the AIC need to be emphasized. First, assessments within this system are enacted within schools precisely because they are taken as the necessary conditions of teaching and learning. In other words, we expect all extensions of teaching and learning are to be assessed or the activity we see them as irrelevant to schooling. The data generated by these ubiquitous assessments are the mark of an activity's legitimacy with the AIC enframed system. Second, all assessments are material enactments—even assumed instructional processes, such as questioning or classroom procedures and routines, become assessments precisely in their ongoing material enactments as "teaching" or "learning." Assessments do not have some original agency, in and of themselves, that can compel, or force, teachers or students to act in specific ways rather than in others. Instead, assessments are precisely already constituted as "teaching" and "learning" within the assessment-driven and AIC-constructed system because they are accepted, or enacted, as the necessary conditions for teachers and students to become what they are supposed to be: college and career ready. Getting to know our students' likes and dislikes, their dreams and ambitions, and their sources of pride and regrets is no longer a humanistic activity undertaken because we care about those we, as teachers, spend our day within the common pursuit of life. These inquiries have become formative assessments, data needed to focus and tailor lessons for maximum impact and effect size as measured by the test.

As such, assessments render some forms of lessons/learning if not impossible, then highly improbable, and others, if not inevitable, then exceedingly likely. Thus, being assessed embodies a particular ontological necessity for the lessons so taught—or differently stated, the teachers and students are the sort of beings that they are because they are always already *enframed* by assessment as such (Heidegger, 1977). Although assessments are the ontological conditions for becoming within contemporary schooling, they are not inevitable as such. When assessments become taken for granted as "teaching" and "learning," they tend to become more or less intractable and irreversible—exactly because they continue to be taken as the ontologically necessary constitutive conditions for teaching and learning. This enframing of education by assessment, through the AIC, is both hegemonic and symbolically violent.

Further, the conceptual frame that characterizes the AICs assessment regime as high-stakes evaluation, grading, and accountability has the dangerous and dehumanizing power of technology. As Heidegger (1977) asserts:

> The essence of technology lies in Enframing. Its holding sway belongs with destining. Since destining at any given time starts man on a way of revealing, man, thus under way, is continually approaching the brink of the possibility of pursuing and pushing forward nothing but what is revealed in ordering, and of deriving all his standards on this basis. Through this the other possibility is blocked, that man might be admitted more and sooner and ever more primally to the essence of that which is unconcealed and to its unconcealment, in order that he might experience as his essence his needed belonging to revealing. (p. 26)

What we care about, where we place priorities, enframes the experiences we have available to us. The danger of the AIC's co-optation and monopolization of assessment is the foreclosure of heterogeneous and empowering learning that is possible in every school and classroom. We do not see common interests, concerns, and passions directed toward our lives as individuals with authentic relationships that emerge within a classroom as legitimate or worthy unless they can produce data that indicates the potential for test score gains.

The Testing Industry and Extension of Agency

Current education policies, both in P–12 education and with growing frequency in higher education, focus upon the commodity value of education and efficiency of schooling. Policies that seek to streamline instruction and curriculum through standards and assessment regimes that hold teachers and schools accountable are dominant within the AIC hegemony (Darling-Hammond, 2006; Dean, Hubbell,

Pitler, & Stone, 2012; Hargreaves & Fullan, 2012; Ladner & Myslinski, 2013; Levine, 2010; McDonald, Kazemi, & Schneider-Kavanagh, 2013; Wagner, 2008). Outcomes of this streamlined and accountable education are seen in the currency of test scores and school league tables (Parkison, 2009). These metrics are meant to provide consumers all the information they require to make "rational" choices about what education to purchase (Apple, 2006; Parkison, 2009). This paradigm, a neoliberal framework that emphasizes college and career readiness as the mantra of purpose and that relies upon the "law of the market" to regulate educational institutions like any other gadget maker, neglects to address the primary stakeholders in education—the learners and their communities.

As educators seek certainty of their efficacy through the development of achievement test scores, they are buying into a paradigm that asserts the existence of an absolute and verifiable world. This basic epistemology is unexamined and problematic. Consider the assumptions of a forced-choice question that provides the primary structure for standardized testing. A forced-choice question offers a learner a set of options that are potential responses to a particular question. There is an assumption of a predetermined, absolutely true answer to the question. Any learner who fails to recognize the correct answer is seen as confused, mistaken, or less proficient. The aspect of the learner as an agent in the construction of meaning through communicative rationality is denied. A forced-choice question does not allow for communicative rationality; interpretation is not given a space within the question, and understanding is not assessed (Parkison, 2006).

Similar claims of certainty and verification are embedded within the standards and assessment policies dominant today. The motivation to become successful in the global economy, as a nation, community, and individual, is center stage (Darling-Hammond, 2010; Wagner, 2008). There is only one aim of life within this paradigm: economic success/viability. The adoption of academic standards began the facilitation and the creation of an education market place founded upon specific and verifiable outcomes with standard objectives, test scores as currency, and competitive opportunities for producers to attract consumers. Those providers who focus on how most efficiently and effectively to achieve standardized outcomes rise based on the law of the market established within AIC's education paradigm.

As states adopt the AIC-constructed assessment systems established within a system of academic standards, they are moving from a system in which curriculum scaffolding is recommended to guide local curriculum development toward a system in which the tests, also based on this scaffolding, become the curriculum. In the early phases of two of the author's careers, local curriculum development was a primary function of teachers as they collaborated in grade-level and instructional teams. We see a prime example in the use of community festivals as a means of generating pride of place and sense of community belonging for middle school students (Parkison, 2006). These local curricula highlighted the diverse and heterogeneous sources of educational experiences that can be generated within schools. As these experiences become marginalized, the normative curriculum of standards, grounded in White, middle class, Christian values, embed the oppressive systems that have structured our history and institutions. Standardized tests become the driving force in the curriculum for states and local education agencies (LEAs). Moreover, people far removed from the lives of those taking the tests and most impacted by them determine the content of these tests.

The politics of the AIC paradigm in education policy and schooling has been dominated by those supporting "college and career readiness" epistemological premises: "It sets up as the norm of all practices, and therefore as ideal rules, the real regularities of the economic world abandoned to its own logic, the so-called laws of the market" (Bourdieu, 1998, p. 35). The language of debate centered upon the aims of life—plurality, diversity, independent self-constitution, self-organization, and ultimately freedom (Havel, 1985)—has been abandoned and has become the language of standards, efficiency, utility, competition, choice, and accountability. High-need schools and the students who attend them, typically individuals who have been marginalized due to race, ethnicity, and socioeconomic status, are *targeted by policy-makers* (officially the target is the achievement gap, or the drop-out rate, or educational inefficiency, or the removal of neglectful administration and teachers) and school-choice and voucher advocates. Zygmunt Bauman's (2007) explanation of the emergence of collateral damage or unintended consequences provides a crucial framework for the critique of these policies:

> The moot question, of course, is whether "unanticipated" means necessarily "impossible to anticipate," and yet more to the point, whether "unintentional" stands for "impossible to calculate" and so "impossible to intentionally avoid," or for a mere indifference and callousness of those who did the calculations and did not care enough about avoiding. Once such a question is explicitly asked, it becomes clear that whatever answer the investigation of a particular case may suggest, there are good reasons to suspect that what the invoking of the "unintentionality" argument intends to deny or exonerate is ethical blindness—conditioned or deliberate. (p. 26)

Within the AIC paradigm, the ethical blindness Bauman identifies is revealed in the proliferation of deficit-laden perspectives that blame the marginalized for being in the wrong place at the wrong time and for making poor (codes include the language of lack of care, motivation, and effort) educational decisions (Apple, 2006; Ayers & Ayers, 2011; Banks, 2007; Delpit, 1995; Gonzalez, Moll, & Amanti, 2005; Ladson-Billings, 2001; Noguera, 2008).

Policies emerging from the AIC paradigm within education portray those who are victimized not as powerless but as ineffective. More faithful adoption and implementation of the standards and preparation for the standardized tests would help these individuals avoid marginalization. Better fidelity to the "college and career readiness" indicators is all that is needed for teachers and schools to be "effective." *They* are the cause of their own marginalization, and they serve as a warning to the rest of "us" that poor decisions potentially threaten the success of all consumers in the education system and place the nation at risk in the global marketplace. We see this enacted in arguments put forward in support of standardized tests like the SAT and ACT. These assessments are suggested as level playing fields in which the marginalized can meritoriously raise themselves through the education system (Nettles & Millett, 2001).

Teachers and students are cast in the underclass because they are seen as totally useless, as a nuisance, pure and simple—something that the rest of us could do nicely without. In the society of consumers—a world that evaluates everyone and everything by their commodity value—they are people with no market value; they are the uncommoditized men and women, and their failure to obtain a status of proper commodity coincides with, (indeed, stems from) their failure to engage in the fully-fledged consumer activity that is contemporary schooling within the AIC hegemony. They are failed consumers—the walking symbols of the disasters that await fallen consumers, and of the ultimate destiny of anyone failing to acquit herself or himself of the consumer duties. (Bauman, 2007). Education and its marginalized stakeholders (students, teachers, and administrators from schools with low test scores) are the threat to the "college and career ready" future and cause of current economic hardships and policy-maker anxiety.

The critical objectives within this neoliberal, law-of-the-market framework are to address raising test scores, reduce achievement gaps, measure response to interventions, and provide differentiated instructional procedures to remediate the failed consumers. Greater fidelity to the "best practice" pedagogy and assessment protocols is primary. Curricula are developed to facilitate equality of capability among students in the mode of consumption that make the paradigm viable in the realm of education (Migone, 2007). Reproduction of prescribed outcomes is the desired result of education.

Accountability Systems in the Context of Teaching and Learning

We have considered the relationships involved in education as the central concern throughout the history and philosophy of education. Teaching and learning, curriculum development, instructional efficacy, accountability, and policy are all viewed within a system of relationships among and between significant stakeholders. As we find ourselves in a place and time, in relation to others, including academic standards and high-stakes testing systems, we bring commitments with us. How we relate to those commitments—political, social, cultural, and economic—determines the power and freedom we have in that context. Prioritizing specific and exclusive commitments, making them ideologically constraining, reduces our generative presence to one of reproduction. If we have not considered the relationships these commitments generate, then we are choosing to continue a state of being for ourselves and the potentialities available to others.

Accountability systems, as developed from within the AIC hegemony, are grounded in a faith in the quantitative measure of student learning and the ability to determine the impact of a teacher's effort statistically. Embedded within this faith are three concerns:

1. A conservatism in the sense that there is a celebration of the American economic, social, and political status quo that is infused with systemic oppression and marginalization;
2. A fear of popular democracy where the non-elite rationalizes non-participation in decision making as necessary to the maintenance and effectiveness of the education system; and
3. An emphasis on rigid assessment methodological principles, models, and elaborate data collection protocols that avoid vital political issues like racial and gender inequalities, poverty, teacher/labor rights, and our national/international welfare in an age of globalization.

Like many spheres of life dominated by neoliberalism, education has rationalized oppressive instrumentalism in the name of being objective, value free, and egalitarian.

The classic political science manuscript "Two Faces of Power" (Bachrach & Baratz, 1962, 1970) and the concept of the mobilization of bias suggest that every political system mobilizes bias in the form of dominant values, cultural symbols, political myths and rituals, and institutional processes. The mobilization of bias in a political system inherently facilitates the organization of some issues into politics, while organizing other issues out of politics. Within education, this same mobilization of bias organizes curricular content into or out of school experiences. By ignoring these selective mechanisms of mobilization of bias, we accept the standards, accountability, and test data as given. To overcome this shortcoming, we propose the necessity of considering the non-curriculum and the perspective of the disempowered with a detailed examination of the specific selective mechanisms of the AIC that mobilizes bias in our educational system to determine their differential impact on the relative power position of different groups (Gaventa, 1980). The relationship between the curriculum and non-curriculum needs to be put into tension.

Considerations of power, structural limitations, and engagement with change help to illuminate the struggle teachers face within the education system as dominated by the AIC. How we respond within the mechanisms of the AIC is constrained by the position we hold within the system—our power or powerlessness places limits on how we interpret educational experiences. Fear of change, engagement in the politics of public spaces like schools, and the struggle between the curriculum and non-curriculum can be understood by considering the instrumental restraints on dialogue. Mikhail Bakhtin (1993) presents the construct of *cosmic terror* that helps to ground the instrumentalization that is so essential to the AIC's hegemony as we unravel it. This concept stresses the radical asymmetry of the struggle between humans and the other (Bakhtin, 1993, 2008) within potential generative dialogue embodied in public spaces. The equal potentiality of stifled dialogue is present within the accountability frameworks associated with the AIC paradigm. *Cosmic terror* plays a key role for Bakhtin in the instrumentalization of fear of change that lives in each event or experience. This fear is also the contextual factor that effectively limits or marginalizes discourse. Within education, we are faced with the critical dilemma of protecting the newness, or innocence, of childhood while also preparing future actors within public and social spaces (Arendt, 1954, 1958; Elshtain, 1995). Understanding *cosmic terror* helps to clarify the obstacles and challenges that need to be engaged to jump toward meaningful, embodied, and generative discourse.

For Bakhtin, dealing with *cosmic terror* implies a re-evaluation of our relationship with the world. For teachers within this frame, it would mean a re-evaluation of our relationship with academic standards, standardized testing, and accountability systems. Bakhtin contrasts two different kinds of relationships: small and great. The *small* register of experiences includes the "secure and stable little world of the family, where nothing is foreign, or accidental or incomprehensible" (Bakhtin, 2008, p. 232). Teachers experience this *small* register relationship in the planning and implementation of lessons aligned to individual standards, indicators, or test items designed for our specific classroom and students. We complete the work of our relationship to standards in each lesson. This register represents a narrow, close-at-hand experience of life, an illusion of permanence and stability erected against the imagination of a broad and abstract world. Teachers experience the *great but abstract* register within the set of academic standards and the aligned standardized tests that hold them accountable within this relationship. The horizon of the *great but abstract* register is a broad vista that draws us out of the comfortable close at hand into the cosmic.

There are two common temptations and potentially adverse outcomes in these registers for those involved in educational pursuits. The first comprises a withdrawal from the greater world through cultivating an unrealistic imagination of education as credentialing. Education is seen as a series of isolated events that accumulate. The absence of these events gets translated as a deficit—either on the part of the learner or on the part of the teacher. Such a state leaves the teacher vulnerable to shock and surprise when the deficit-laden *other-for-me* is present in the learning setting. The second danger follows from this, in that the teacher makes themselves susceptible to forces that promise to maintain or return stability by remediating the deficit. Bakhtin (2008) observed that to the person who inhabits *small experiences* there is one cognizer (everything else is an object of cognition), one who is living and unclosed (everything else is unresponsively dead and closed), and one who speaks (everything else is unresponsively silent). In Bakhtin's view of *great experiences,* everything is alive and speaks.

Withdrawal from the *great world* does not have a liberating or protective effect, but, instead, makes the individual more manageable and controllable. Where one equates loss of stability with loss of meaning, there is a will to give over control

(Gaventa, 1980). Academic standards and high stakes accountability or standardized assessment systems gesture toward an "official culture" by creating the illusion of maintaining control, and this *official culture* gains power by nourishing a desire for a stable environment. Indicating the role of *official culture* (Bakhtin, 1984, p. 336), Bakhtin demonstrates how power is achieved and maintained by addressing our desire for an unchanging environment or context, a focus on the close at hand and *small experiences*. The academic standards play this role when treated as objects that perform. We can see this in the move to Common Core State Standards (CCSS) and the standardized testing that accompanies them (Knoester & Parkison, 2017; Parkison, 2015). In a review of the development of CCSS, Lavenia et al. (2015) argue that the adoption of CCSS is linked to policy termination. This policy effectively ends dialogue and provides a stable *small experience* set of guidelines for states and schools. Bakhtin finds that human awareness needs to stretch further than one's immediate surroundings to understand one's situatedness. While the shortsighted view of *small experience* only allows us to see the immediate destruction and personal loss, and the *great experiences* make us desire an unrealistic conception of meaning, Bakhtin's alternative contextualizes our relationship to everything else.

Navigating the AIC

While this text intends to unravel and expose the underlying motives and outcomes of the AIC against these various theoretical frameworks, we hope to offer a credible critique of its impact on students, teachers, and society. In each chapter, we also focus on the rhetoric of the AIC to expose how proponents of education reform utilize language to normalize and legitimize the value of tests and the data extracted from them to justify their ideological agenda. In the forthcoming chapters, we examine the limitations of the AIC and offer potential solutions.

In Chapter 1, *Introducing the Assessment Industrial Complex: How This Book Came to Be*, as authors and educators committed to equality and social justice, we position ourselves and our experiences with the AIC and ground our analysis in the framework of "neoliberalism," illustrating its association with the AIC. We provide a thorough explanation of the "Assessment Industrial Complex" and the issues that accompany this hegemonic paradigm. We conclude by discussing some of our primary concerns with the AIC: How the AIC disproportionately impacts our most vulnerable students has been a primary motivation for this project.

In Chapter 2, *Testing and Society: How We Got to Where We Are*, we investigate the history of testing in the United States and consider the implications of testing as a gatekeeper both within and beyond the schooling context. We utilize Kendi's (2019) antiracist lens to demonstrate the racist nature of standardized testing in the United States. Chapter 2 concludes by providing a brief history of neoliberalism in US policy, which provides historical context for the bipartisan support of the AIC throughout the last four decades.

Chapter 3, *Strange Bedfellows: How Test-Driven Accountability Became Common Sense* explores the amalgamation of corporate profits and political interests and examines the rhetoric that promotes the idea of standardized testing as a matter of national security, economic survival, and social justice. Tracing the consolidation of the AIC's power from *A Nation at Risk* through *No Child Left Behind* and to *Race to the Top* illustrates how the enframing of education has occurred. The chapter further demonstrates the capacity of rhetoric to manipulate policy-makers to form bipartisan education policy and justify their actions via the AIC.

Chapter 4, *Testing for Profit: Billionaire Boys' Club, EdReformers and All Matter of Money*, describes how the AIC operates, which includes an examination of EdReformers and their role in shaping and contributing to the AIC. More specifically, we focus on how these influential stakeholders utilize money and influence to inform education policy and shift educational practices that benefit the AIC and disadvantage our most vulnerable students. We analyze major billionaires' and edu-philanthropists' influence on all aspects of education while exposing the hypocrisy of their claims in the face of the material reality of the outcomes of their actions.

Chapter 5, *Students, Teachers, and Testing: An Existential Crisis in the Making*, focuses on the relationship between corporations' desire to manufacture profits via assessments to the detriment of students, especially the most vulnerable students that these reforms promised to help. Testing within today's schools is ubiquitous. We explore current trends in testing and the ripple effects it has had on students' and teachers' lives. We also address the COVID-19 crisis and what it reveals about the AIC and education decision making.

Finally, in Chapter 6, *A Path to Hope and Change: The Time is Now,* we explore current anti-testing movements and demonstrate how they are disrupting the AIC. We discuss the COVID-19 pandemic and exemplify some impacts it is having on high-stakes, standardized testing. The pandemic has opened a door, providing us the opportunity to walk through it and dismantle the AIC. But the door will undoubtedly close if our society does nothing. Hence, we call for actions, ones that will hopefully lead to the abolishment of the AIC.

References

Apple, M. (2006). *Educating the "right" way: Markets, standards, God, and inequality* (2nd ed.). London, UK: Routledge

Arendt, H. (1954). *Between past and future: Eight exercises in political thought.* New York, NY: Penguin Books.

Arendt, H. (1958). *The human condition.* Chicago, IL: The University of Chicago Press.

ASCD. (April, 2020). A new reality: Getting remote learning right. *Educational Leadership, 77.* Retrieved from http://www.ascd.org/Publications/Educational-Leadership/EL-Download.aspx.

Ayers, R., & Ayers, W. (2011). *Teaching the Taboo: Courage and Imagination in the Classroom.* New York, NY: Teachers College Press.

Bachrach, P., & Baratz, M. (1962). The two faces of power. *American Political Science Review, 56,* 947–952.

Bachrach, P., & Baratz, M. (1970). *Power and poverty: Theory and practice.* Oxford, UK: Oxford University Press.

Bakhtin, M. (1984). *Rabelais and his world.* Bloomington: Indiana University Press.

Bakhtin, M. (1993). In V. Lianpov & M. Holquist (Eds.), *Toward a philosophy of the act.* Austin: University of Texas Press.

Bakhtin, M. (2008). *The dialogic imagination.* Austin: University of Texas Press.

Banks, J. A. (2007). *Educating citizens in a multicultural society* (2nd ed.). New York, NY: Teachers College Press.

Bauman, Z. (2007). Collateral casualties of consumerism, *Journal of Consumer Culture, 7*(1), 25–56.

Bourdieu, P. (1998). *Acts of resistance: Against the tyranny of the market.* New York, NY: Free Press.

Conn, D. R., & Tenam-Zemach, M. (2019). Educational fronts for local and global justice confronting the assessment industrial complex: A call for a shift from testing rhetoric. *Special Issue of Journal of Curriculum Theorizing: Curriculum Theorizing in the Post-Truth Era, 34*(3), 122–135.

Darling-Hammond, L. (2006). Assessing teacher education: The usefulness of multiple measures for assessing program outcomes. *Journal of Teacher Education, 57*(2), 120–138.

Darling-Hammond, L. (2010). *The flat world and education: How 'America's commitment to equity will determine our future.* New York, NY: Teachers College Press.

Dean, C., Hubbell, E., Pitler, H., & Stone, B. (2012). *Classroom instruction that works: Research-based strategies for increasing student achievement.* Alexandria, VA: Pearson Teacher Education/Association for Supervision and Curriculum Development.

Deleuze, G. G., & Guattari, F. F. (1987). *A thousand plateaus: Capitalism and schizophrenia.* New York, NY: Continuum.

Delpit, L. (1995). *Other people's children: Cultural conflict in the classroom.* New York, NY: The New Press.

Elshtain, J. B. (1995). Political children. In B. Honig (Ed.), *Feminist interpretations of Hannah Arendt* (pp. 263–285). University Park: The University of Pennsylvania Press.

Gaventa, J. (1980). *Power and powerlessness: Quiescence and rebellion in an Appalachian valley.* Urbana: University of Illinois Press.

Gonzalez, N., Moll, L. C., & Amanti, D. (2005). *Funds of knowledge: Theorizing practices in household, communities, and classrooms.* Mahwah, NJ: Lawrence Erlbaum Associates, Publishers.

Hargreaves, A., & Fullan, M. (2012). *Professional capital: Transforming teaching in every school.* New York, NY: Teachers College Press.

Havel, V. (1985). The power of the powerless. In J. Keane (Ed.), *The power of the powerless: Citizens against the state in Central-Eastern Europe* (pp. 23–96). Armonk, NY: M.E. Sharpe.

Heidegger, M. (1977). *The question concerning technology, and other essays* (W. Levitt Trans.). New York, NY: Harper & Row.

Kendi, I. X. (2019). *How to be an antiracist.* New York, NY: Random House.

Kenigsberg Levi, S. (2020, March 20). *This angry mom's rant about homeschooling children while in quarantine goes viral.* [Video File]. Retrieved from https://www.youtube.com/watch?v=H7_wvQHMGOI.

Knoester, M., & Parkison, P. (2017). Seeing like a state: How educational policy misreads what is important in schools. *Educational Studies, 53*(3), 247–262.

Krasinski, J. (2020, March 29). *Some good news with John Krasinski Ep. 1 [Video file].* Retrieved from https://www.youtube.com/watch?v=oilZ1hNZPRM&t=364s.

Ladner, M. & Myslinski, D.. (2013). *Report card on American education: Ranking state K-12 performance, progress, and reform.* Washington, DC: American Legislative Exchange Council.

Ladson-Billings, G. (2001). *Crossing over to Canaan: The journey of new teachers in diverse classrooms.* New York, NY: Jossey-Bass.

Lavenia, M., Cohen-Vogel, L., & Lang, L. B. (2015). The Common Core State Standards initiative: An event history analysis of state adoption. *American Journal of Education, 121*(2), 145–182.

Levine, A. (2010). Teacher education must respond to changes in America. *Kappan, 92*(2), 19–24.

Long, C. (2020, March 19). Parents-turned-homeschoolers agree: Teachers are amazing! *neaToday.* Retrieved from http://neatoday.org/2020/03/19/homeschooling-during-coronavirus-outbreak/.

McDonald, M., Kazemi, E., & Schneider-Kavanagh, S. (2013, November). Core practices and pedagogies of teacher education: A call for a common language and collective activity. *Journal of Teacher Education, 64*(5), 378–386.

Migone, A. (2007). Hedonistic consumerism: Patterns of consumption in contemporary capitalism. *Review of Radical Political Economics, 39*(2), 173–200.

Mulvenon, S. W., Stegman, C. E., & Ritter, G. (2005). Test anxiety: A multifaceted study on the perceptions of teachers, principals, counselors, students, and parents. *International Journal of Testing, 5*(1), 37–61.

Nettles, M. T., & Millett, C. M. (2001). Toward diverse student representation and higher achievement in higher levels of the American educational meritocracy. In B. D. Smedley, Y. Stith, L. Colburn & C. H. Evans (Eds.), *The right thing to do, the smart thing to do — Summary of the symposium of diversity in the health professions in honor of W. Nickens, M. D.* (pp. 143–184). New York, NY: National Academy Press: Institute of Medicine.

Noguera, P. A. (2008). *The trouble with Black Boys: And other reflections on race, equity, and the future of public education.* San Francisco, CA: Jossey-Bass.

Parkison, P. (2006). The community festival as a teachable moment. *Middle Ground: The Magazine of Middle Level Education, 39*(2), 135–148.

Parkison, P. (2009). Political economy of NCLB: Standards, testing and test scores. *The Educational Forum, 73*(1), 44–57.

Parkison, P. (2015). Catharsis in education: Rationalizing and reconciling. *Journal of Curriculum and Teaching Dialogue, 17*(2), 121–136.

Perelman, D. (2020, July 2). In the Covid-19 economy, you can have a kid or a job. You can't have both. *New York Times.* Retrieved from https://www.nytimes.com/2020/07/02/business/covid-economy-parents-kids-career-homeschooling.html.

Roberts, M. A. (2015). The testing industrial complex: Incarcerating education since 2001. In M. Abendroth & B. J. Porfilio (Eds.), *Understanding neoliberal rule in K-12 schools:educational fronts for local and global justice* (pp. 153–180). Chicago, IL: IAP.

Shropshire, B. (2020, March 18). *A desperate mothers' prayer.* [Video File]. Retrieved from https://www.youtube.com/watch?v=gpN9CGrK6IQ.

The Upside Down. (n.d.). *Fandom.* Retrieved from https://strangerthings.fandom.com/wiki/The_Upside_Down.

Wagner, T. (2008). *The global achievement gap.* New York, NY: Basic Books.

Westheimer, J. (2020, March 31). Forget trying to be your kid's substitute teacher during CoVid. *Ottawa Citizen.* Retrieved from https://ottawacitizen.com/opinion/westheimer-forget-trying-to-be-your-kids-substitute-school-teacher-during-covid-19.

1

INTRODUCING THE ASSESSMENT INDUSTRIAL COMPLEX

How This Book Came to Be

Each of us began our journey in the education system at different points in time, even as early as the 1990s, a time before or at the emergence of "hyper-standardization, hyperaccountability, and neoliberal school reform" (Royal & Gibson, 2017, p. 1). We recall a time when testing was not the raison d'etre of education and the focus of classroom activities. So we understand the parallel right-side-up world that focused on human relationships in the classroom and student learning, what it looked and felt like, and what our purpose as educators was. None of this implies that schools before hyperstandardization were perfect. Students of color were ignored, as were those who had learning disabilities, and equity was not a common term associated with the system of education (Ravitch, 2001). Tests were implemented, and the data were not always used to serve all students. Nevertheless, as Koretz (2017) reminds us, "Our heavy-handed use of tests for accountability has also undermined precisely the function that testing is best designed to serve: providing trustworthy information about student achievement" (p. 6).

Moreover, curriculum and assessment have a unique and intriguing relationship. As complex assemblages on their own, when viewed in interaction, the relationship creates a field of education that is dynamic, heterogeneous, and transformative. Fundamentally the idea of complex assemblages is that there does not exist a fixed and stable ontology for schooling and education that proceeds from "atoms" to "molecules" to "materials." Instead, social formations are assemblages of other complex configurations, and they, in turn, play roles in other, more extended configurations. Deleuze and Guattari (1987) provide a strategy for considering the "line of flight or deterritorialization" (p. 89) of these assemblages. As complex systems (assemblages), we can consider the interminglings of their components in defining education: the component of the school and the student body; the components of teachers and administrators and those of the students and parents; the components of the district and state administrators and those of the state policy-makers and the assessment industry; the body of state academic standards and the body of the high-stakes assessments and accountability metrics; the "weapons and tools assuring a symbiosis of bodies—a whole machinic of assemblages" (Deleuze & Guattari, 1987, p. 89).

It would be an error to assert that academic standards determine the school curriculum in some causal relation or interaction. Academic standards are not powerful enough to even reflect the curriculum as enacted. What regulates the interaction and intermingling of academic standards and the curriculum is the high-stakes testing and accountability regimes. When a standards-aligned lesson is taught, the heterogeneity of the students' and teacher's experiences enters the lesson along with the standardized content. Tests are meant to reign in this diversity. Even a technologic or instrumental view of assessment makes a mistake if it considers the tool—the tests themselves—in isolation. The tests only exist in relation to the interminglings they make possible, or that make them possible. Tests are inseparable from the amalgamations that define schooling and education within the machinic assemblage of the Assessment Industrial Complex (AIC) hegemony. The AIC not only produces, sells, and distributes the tests, but it embodies the ideology of the powerful. Curriculum becomes constrained by the functioning of the tests. The tool has been assigned inappropriate attributes that have come to anchor schooling, education, and the curriculum to them. The relationship is reversed in this amalgamation. Curriculum has become the tool of assessment.

Through this relationship, the test determines what should be taught and takes on the dominant role. For example, the "backwards design" model (Wiggins & McTighe, 2005) calls for curriculum to focus on standards, objectives, and assessment. Although this may not have been the intent of Wiggins et al., school districts have used this framework to drive curriculum decisions around students' standardized test scores. Au (2007), for example, found

> a significant relationship between the implementation of high stakes testing and changes in the content of a curriculum, the structure of knowledge contained within the content, and the types of pedagogy associated with communication of that content. These changes represent three types of control that high-stakes tests exert on curriculum: content control, formal control, and pedagogic control. (p. 262)

This relationship imposes what and how teachers teach. Consequently, teachers must now design their curriculum and base their curricular decisions on items that they anticipate will be on the test and to primarily focus on improving upon deficits according to the testing data. This relationship is problematic for a variety of reasons, and we explore some of these reasons throughout the book. Still, it is especially problematic that a test determines what we should teach without first attending to the cultural and pedagogical needs of the students. This implies what we choose to test matters more than the students themselves.

Despite the number of years we as educators have been involved in the field of education, we nonetheless shudder at the examples of abuse and emotional and symbolic violence (Bourdieu, 1979; Saltman, 2018) testing has brought to stakeholders in our education system and society. According to Saltman (2018), symbolic violence is "the devaluation of one's culture, knowledge, language tastes, and disposition" (p. 113). Historically, these elements were the foundation of curriculum development, but now, standardized testing determines what does and does not constitute as valued knowledge. The test provides boilerplate answers, within a dialogic vacuum, to critical questions of what should be taught and learned in schools. As such, high-stakes testing imposes symbolic violence by reifying forms of knowledge that benefit those in power while oppressing and marginalizing cultures and devaluing their knowledge. The sense of powerlessness also leads to greater susceptibility to the internalization of the values, beliefs, or rules of the game of the powerful as an adaptive response—as a means of escaping the subjective sense of powerlessness, if not its objective condition (Gaventa, 1980). Saltman (2018) further points out:

> The student is thus made complicit in her own cultural oppression. This is a cultural oppression that has material effects: the sorting and sifting techniques of the school such as testing are used to position students to do different work and to have different things. (p. 7)

To further exemplify this, Koretz (2017) narrates a scenario where, focusing on test scores, some schools post "data walls" that indicate the performance of students on practice exams utilized to prepare students for their state's inevitable end-of-year exam. When we reduce the person—each student—to a data point, we dehumanize all children who function within this system. Even those who are "high achieving" are reduced to a data point. Educators strip away the humanity of education in the name of testing. One student, in particular, that Koretz (2017) discussed, traced a row of dots that indicated her scores on the various state standards on her most recent practice tests. "Red, red, yellow, red, green, red. Janie is a child capable of much drama, but that morning she just lowered her gaze to the floor and shuffled to her chair..." (p. 2). Koretz (2017) further states that,

> Even an adult faced with a row of red dots after her name for all her peers to see would have to dig deep into her hard-won sense of self to put into context what those red dots meant in her life and what she would do about them. An eight-year-old just feels shame. (p. 2)

This example demonstrates the face of symbolic violence foisted on students whose sense of self is utterly devalued via the symbolism of colored dots. These dots encapsulate a student's value as determined by an unjust and culturally oppressive system. On a human level, just reading these words evokes pain, and anyone who has lived the life of a teacher, student, or parent knows that this should not occur in the hallowed halls of schools. Another outrageous example Koretz documents focuses on a first-grade teacher, Kim Cook, who works in Alachua County, Florida. She was voted Teacher of the Year in 2012–2013. At the time, the state did not administer its state's high-stakes annual exam, the Florida Comprehensive Assessment Test (FCAT), in the first grade. Since her school enrolls students only from preschool through second grade, the school board determined that her evaluation would be based on 40% of the "test scores of fourth- and fifth-grade students in *another school*" (p. 3). Cook and several others were part of a group of plaintiffs that sued the Florida commissioner of education. As Koretz points out, "They lost." (p. 3). Strauss (2019) revisits two of the most "absurd and appalling" (paragraph 1) stories that were an outcome of the relentless focus on standardized testing during the 2010s. In the first story, she narrates an event that occurred in 2013 when Florida's DOE required a nine-year-old boy, Michael, who was missing a part of his brain, to take a version of the FCAT. Michael was both blind and mute and could not comprehend basic information. Yet, according to the Florida DOE, every child must be evaluated and sit for the test. Michael was forced to take the test, which, according to Strauss, meant that someone had to actually sit down and read to him the contents of the test. The second incident involved a boy named Ethan, whose parents were forced to not only request a waiver for the FCAT, but they also had to prove that their son deserved it even though he was in a morphine coma and dying.

While these incidents underscore the irrationality underlying the AIC, the most oft-cited data related to the evaluation of schools and their outcomes are standardized test scores. Standardized tests are "maps" that policy-makers use to simplify the complex organizations that are public schools and the knowledge of the living human beings that spend a large portion of their time in them. In the practitioner experience of education and schooling, change and uncertainty, unpredictability, and instability prevail. There is an ever-increasing need for capacities of self-organization and adaptability. Yet, education policy relentlessly pursues standardization, compliance, and accountability, sometimes even at the expense of dying children and their families.

Additionally, testing disproportionately harms our most vulnerable students in severe and enduring ways. For example, Goodman (2018) points out something well-known in the field of language acquisition: English Language Learners (ELLs), who often have experienced multiple forms of trauma, struggle with achieving academic language proficiency, on average, for 5–10 years. Yet, they are forced to take high-stakes tests in an "environment that is unforgiving to newcomers and their particular challenges. They score an average of 20–50 percentage points below their native-English-speaking peers…" (p. 58). As Goodman notes throughout his book, many ELL students originate from countries where extreme violence and suffering occur, and these students are often traumatized as a result of their experiences. Despite their trauma, our current requirements for testing in public schools are immune to considering these realities and, thus, further traumatize students through forms of symbolic violence that are the demands of hyper-accountability and the testing regime.

One of the authors of this text personally attests to the pain and suffering testing has caused her family. One of her sons recently spent the majority of his junior year in high school studying for the SAT exam in preparation for his college applications. While a strong student academically—he graduated top 2% of his high school class—standardized testing is not one of his perceived strengths. This is incredibly frustrating given that one of his siblings is a "natural" test taker, and the other's performance correlates with his effort spent prepping for standardized tests (see Koretz, 2017, *Testing Charade* for an interesting analysis on Test Prep). We will forgo a discussion of why a parent who understands the lack of value of these tests would still allow her child to suffer the indignation and torture of studying for them. More frustrating is that she knows studying for these tests will waste her son's precious time and lead to nothing productive other than sorting and ranking her child for college admissions (and she does NOT consider this a productive but an evil necessity). The purpose of this anecdote is to demonstrate that, despite her knowledge of the powerful neoliberal forces that control the education system, she too feels helpless to challenge the system at the cost of her son's college aspirations.

In understanding how symbolic violence functions, even the most educated parents are subject to its pernicious effects, as this author's experiences demonstrate. The author is complicit in the devaluation of her knowledge and recognizes this material effect; yet, despite understanding her conflict, she persisted in providing her son the tools and means to have access and opportunity through the college admissions process. And there are additional problems that she recognizes as well. First is the damage this test has done to her son's self-efficacy, self-esteem, sense of purpose of education, and understanding of his value and place in the sorting machine of college admissions. Second, and this is an even larger problem, she recognizes her complicity in contributing to the inequity and injustice in our society. Ultimately, the realities of our current college admissions process are clearly counter-productive not only to our children but also to our society as a whole.

As many narratives as we can find that underscore the negative impacts of testing, in particular, high-stakes testing (the central focus of this book), one must wonder why it persists. Why have we, as a society, accepted that standardized tests, with all their problems and adverse effects, persist as the final arbiter and measure of success? It could not only be because they appear, falsely so, to be objective; that would not account for the abusive manner in which they are administered and utilized (Koretz, 2017; Zhao, 2018). It could not possibly be because the data can be easily manipulated by proponents of testing and sold to the public as honest, "objective" measures of students' achievement. If this were the case, parents in New York and other states would not be outraged by their children being pawns in their school districts' abuse of their children. This is one reason why many parents engage in various opt-out testing movements (Strauss, 2018). It could not be because we, as a society, believe that drilling students on test items reflects our belief in the purpose of education. Forty-five percent of respondents on the 2016 PDK Poll of the Public's Attitudes Toward the Public schools do not agree on the purpose of education, much less that testing is that purpose (Phi Delta Kappan, 2017). And even though this list of why it "could not be" can continue indefinitely, perhaps it is something far more deceptively simple: testing generates a great deal of money and power for those controlling the system of education.

The way the rhetoric of the AIC is produced and controlled disempowers stakeholders and mediates their relationship to the educational system in ways that reinforce and legitimize the AIC. The relationship between public opinion and policies related to testing in education is framed within a reciprocal dialogue between consciousness and participation. The constructs used within the narrative of education enframe stakeholder consciousness and ring-fence the means of participation in the system. Quiescence to this rhetoric is evident in the consistent reference to test scores, achievement gaps, and standards. It is essential to recognize that this impacts the powerful and powerless alike. This is well understood in an overtly political context: consciousness promotes participation, and in its turn, participation increases consciousness. If the second understanding of the relationship to participation and consciousness is the case, then it should also be the case that those who are denied participation—like teachers and students in the curriculum planning and development process—also might not develop consciousness of their situation or of the broader inequalities. Paulo Freire developed this relationship of non-participation to non-consciousness of deprived or oppressed groups stating, "consciousness is constituted in the dialectic of man's objectification and action upon the world" (Freire, 1972, p. 52).

Neoliberalism: A Definition

The term "Neoliberalism" has "multiple and contradictory meanings" that stretches across an array of disciplines (Venugopal, 2015, p. 165). Venugopal expands on these contradictions: "Largely as a result of this growing conceptual ambiguity, neoliberalism is now widely acknowledged in the literature as a controversial, incoherent, and crisis-ridden term, even by many of its most influential deployers" (p. 165). Despite the ambiguity of the term, neoliberalism offers a potential theoretical framework to analyze and understand the current systemic inequities that are extant in society and the system of education specifically. Martinez and Garcia (1997) provide a comprehensive definition that includes five main points of neoliberalism:

1. THE RULE OF THE MARKET. Liberating "free" enterprise or private enterprise from any bonds imposed by the government (the state) no matter how much social damage this causes. Greater openness to international trade and investment, as in NAFTA. Reduce wages by de-unionizing workers and eliminating workers' rights that had been won over many years of struggle... total freedom of movement for capital, goods and services.

2. CUTTING PUBLIC EXPENDITURE FOR SOCIAL SERVICES like education and health care. REDUCING THE SAFETY-NET FOR THE POOR, and even maintenance of roads, bridges, water supply—again in the name of reducing government's role. Of course, they don't oppose government subsidies and tax benefits for business.

3. DEREGULATION. Reduce government regulation of everything that could diminish profits, including protecting the environment and safety on the job.

4. PRIVATIZATION. Sell state-owned enterprises, goods and services to private investors. This includes banks, key industries, railroads, toll highways, electricity, schools, hospitals and even fresh water...privatization has mainly had the effect of concentrating wealth even more in a few hands and making the public pay even more for its needs.

5. ELIMINATING THE CONCEPT OF "THE PUBLIC GOOD" or "COMMUNITY" and replacing it with "individual responsibility." Pressuring the poorest people in a society to find solutions to their lack of health care, education and social security all by themselves—then blaming them, if they fail, as "lazy" (paragraphs 8–12).

Historically, neoliberalism was popularized through easy-to-understand metaphors and antidotes by conservative voices like Ayn Rand, Milton Friedman, and the presidency of Ronald Reagan. Through these and other empowered advocates of neoliberalism, it has become one of the most pervasive and dangerous ideologies of the 21st century. Its pervasiveness is evident not only by its unparalleled influence on the global economy but also in its power to redefine the very nature of politics and society. As Noam Chomsky (2017) notes

> It's [neoliberalism] not called that. What it's called is 'freedom,' but 'freedom' means a subordination to the decisions of concentrated, unaccountable, private power. That's what it means. The institutions of governance—or other kinds of association that could allow people to participate in decision making—those are systematically weakened. Margaret Thatcher said it rather nicely in her aphorism about 'there is no society, only individuals.'
>
> *(paragraph 15)*

Thus, it is the individual who becomes disconnected from the collective who then becomes unable to take action against that which oppresses it. Citing Marx,

Chomsky points out that "the repression is turning society into a sack of potatoes, just individuals, an amorphous mass can't act together" (Lydon, June 2, 2017, paragraph 16). Further, free-market fundamentalism, aka neoliberalism, is the driving force of economics and politics in most of the world. Its logic has insinuated itself into every social relationship, such that the specificity of relations between parents and children, doctors and patients, teachers and students, for example, has been reduced to that of supplier and customer.

The public education system in the U.S. has been laid to waste as a result of neoliberal policies and rhetoric that we discuss throughout the chapters of this book. From the federal to state and local levels, policies that have been enacted as a result of reports like *A Nation at Risk* (1983), have dramatically reduced students', parents', and teachers' influence over the system of education. This reduction of influence, and thus participation, create situations of highly unequal power relationships, which are essentially closed societies in which the interests and outcomes are no longer contested, and the powerless become highly dependent. They are prevented from either self-determined actions or reflection upon their actions. Denied the dialectical process of the development of educational participation and consciousness and denied the democratic experience out of which critical consciousness grows, teachers, students, and often parents develop a culture of silence. The culture of silence precludes the development of consciousness amongst the disempowered or powerless, thus lending the powerful, the AIC, an air of legitimacy. As in the sense of powerlessness, it may also encourage a susceptibility among the dependent society to internalization of the values of the dominant group themselves. Since teachers, students, and often parents have been socialized into compliance, they accept the definitions of educational reality as offered by the dominant group in the form of the AICs hegemony.

This shift also created a space for proponents of education reform to reframe the narrative around the need for greater accountability leading to the commodification of education. This commodification opened the floodgates for corporations and other businesses to profit from the education system. High-stakes testing and other forms of assessments became the most expedient method to hold the system, and everyone involved in it, accountable, thus becoming the driving force of all education decision making and profiteering. As a result, current education policies under the assessment driven education system, both in P-12 education and with growing frequency in higher education, focus upon the commodity value of education and efficiency of schooling. Policies that seek to streamline instruction and curriculum through assessment and accountability regimes that hold teachers and schools accountable are dominant (Darling-Hammond, 2006; Dean, Hubbell, Hargreaves & Fullan, 2012; Ladner & Myslinski, 2013; Levine, 2010; McDonald, Kazemi, & Schneider-Kavanagh, 2013; Pitler & Stone, 2012; Wagner, 2008).

Koretz (2017), chronicles the "failures of test-based accountability" (p. 8) and refers to the current usage of tests as absurd and causing real harm. Thus, while education reform is nothing new in the United States, the emphasis on high-stakes testing is an experiment with devastating consequences for our students, schools, and society. It is challenging, therefore, to understand why we continue down what seems to be a destructive and dangerous path. As we began to investigate the underpinnings of the testing and assessment regime, we found one construct to help explain why society continues in this direction: assessment, similar to the military, prison, and other industrial complexes, has become its own industrial complex. Thus, we henceforth refer to this construct as the "AIC."

What Is the Assessment Industrial Complex?

Origins

To understand the Assessment Industrial Complex, we begin by describing the "military industrial complex" (MIC). Dwight D. Eisenhower committed a lifetime of public service, which included leadership as a five star general in the U.S. Army, Supreme Commander of the Allied Expeditionary Forces, Supreme Commander of the North Atlantic Treaty Organization (NATO), and eight years as President of the United States. After his service, he delivered a stern warning, in his farewell address, about the unwarranted influence of the armament industry on public policy:

> In the councils of government, we must guard against the acquisition of unwarranted influence, whether sought or unsought, by the military-industrial complex. The potential for the disastrous rise of misplaced power exists and will persist.

> We must never let the weight of this combination endanger our liberties or democratic processes. We should take nothing for granted. Only an alert and knowledgeable citizenry can compel the proper meshing of the huge industrial and military machinery of defense with our peaceful methods and goals, so that security and liberty may prosper together.
>
> *(Eisenhower, 1961, p. 15)*

Since Eisenhower's warning of the military-industrial complex, the U.S. has fought historically long, controversial, and costly wars in Vietnam, Afghanistan, and Iraq. This is evidenced by the sheer number of dollars the U.S. has expended since his warning. For example, the U.S. spent 598 billion dollars in 2016, which accounts for one-third of all military spending in the world (Taylor & Karklis, 2016).

As U.S. military spending has increased over this time, the military industry has undoubtedly profited. Lockheed Martin, Halliburton, Boeing, and other corporations received generous and even exclusive contracts to provide supplies for defense, war, and rebuilding infrastructure after wars. Consequently, when these corporations attempt to sell weapons of war to the federal government, congressional representatives have more than just lobbying dollars and their investments to sway votes toward paying inflated costs for weaponry. These weapon purchases can also translate to jobs for individual states and congressional districts. For example, in 2009, Lockheed Martin offered the U.S. Government Stealth F-22 Raptor fighter jets for $350 million per plane. The plane is advertised as the first and only "27/7/365 All-Weather Stealth Fighter" with a "radar signature the size of a bumblebee" (Hartung, 2010, p. 2). When Rep. John Murtha (D-PA), Rep. Jerry Lewis (R-CA), Defense Secretary Robert Gates, and military officials suggested the price was far too high, Lockheed Martin lobbied Congress; they even paid for advertisements to sway the American public. Sen. Saxby Chambliss (R-GA), Joseph Lieberman (I-CT), and Chris Dodd (D-CT), a bi-partisan group, were especially vocal in support for paying the sticker price for the fighter jets, with manufacturing plants to build F-22 engines for Lockheed Martin in Connecticut and Georgia. As a debate ensued over the cost of F-22s, the late Sen. John McCain (R-AZ) quoted Eisenhower's military-industrial complex reference and went on to note Congress's culpable role in the complex (Hartung, 2010).

While individual senators and representatives might be able to rationalize paying inflated prices for the most advanced weaponry because of their position that it increases the safety of U.S. citizens, and they are equating this cost to jobs for their constituents, it is troubling to realize that these military-industrial corporations can so easily gouge the American public and even affect policy toward on-going wars. Furthermore, the military-industrial complex has also affected other aspects of society, which include arming local police departments with military weapons (Kraska, 2007) and the rise of other industrial complexes, like the prison industrial complex (Sudbury, 2014). Although U.S. policymakers have primarily ignored Eisenhower's warning, the material reality of the military-industrial complex has yielded a series of perpetual wars for the past six decades (Chomsky, 1999, 2017; Ledbetter, 2011). While these consequences of the military-industrial complex are certainly worth further examination, we focus our critique back to the Assessment Industrial Complex.

Assessment Industrial Complex

Spring and Picciano (2013) originated the concept of the "educational industrial complex" (p. 2) wherein they discuss the influence of corporate and political interests on public school and their damaging effects. The AIC fuses several different interests—political, social, and corporate—to form a power bloc that enframes, defines, and encapsulates the contexts and experiences of students, teachers, and schools. A multitude of educational businesses and corporations' attempt to shape educational policy to generate large profits, and, conversely, policymakers rely on the data from standardized tests to legitimize their policies (Au, 2011; Saltman, 2012). This reciprocal relationship ensures that corporations, politicians, and other entities will contribute to and support politicians' campaigns and reinforce the status quo in terms of who remains in power. Additionally, while the discourse of policymakers offers the illusion that student education outcomes are relevant, and the significant investments made in public education reflect that belief, a large chunk of those funds are channeled to the assessment industry (Parkison, 2015; Picciano, 1994; Spring & Picciano, 2013; Strauss, 2013).

Furthermore, despite the rhetoric that claims that education policies and reforms are serving the public good, in reality, they are increasingly damaging the public schools they vow to support. Simultaneously, many proponents of testing intentionally and systematically mislead the American public about what the testing data indicates. For example, Betsy DeVos, the Secretary of Education under the Trump administration, assailed the 2019 NAEP results. Yet, she did not mention the implementation of the Common Core State Standards in 2010, the overemphasis on standardized testing at the expense of instruction and interdisciplinary teaching, and other education reforms like online reading instruction as possible causes for the national decline in test scores (Green & Goldstein, 2019).

Ravitch (2013), echoing the work of Spring and Picciano (2013), utilized the term Education Industrial Complex when describing the dovetailed relationship of various entities, including government agencies, philanthropies, businesses, and organizations. She argues that such entities work toward the privatization of education and focus on high-stakes testing as a means of achieving their ends. Saltman (2018) aligns his argument with Ravitch's stating,

> Schools and districts have come to be increasingly modeled on corporate culture…teachers need to deliver numerically measurable results…curriculum and pedagogy are increasingly standardized, and schools must 'compete' against each other for test scores to secure federal funding while parents are described as 'consumers…' (p. xiv)

If an increased emphasis on standardized testing is a step in the wrong direction, the AIC has taken us further and faster off course. When *No Child Left Behind* (NCLB) was first enacted, students began taking high-stakes standardized tests in 3rd grade (Thomas & Brady, 2005); now, they are taking high-stakes standardized tests in preschool. Students take standardized tests more frequently, as well. Because summative standardized testing has such dramatic consequences for students, teachers, schools, districts, and states, an increasing number of students are subjected to "formative" standardized testing to monitor student progress toward achievement on the summative, high-stakes assessment. Today in the U.S., for example, young people will take an average of 112 standardized tests before they graduate from high school (Hart et al., 2015). Yet, despite all these tests, it is difficult to say that we, as a society, are better off. Notwithstanding all this talk about closing the achievement gap, socioeconomic mobility is stagnant for too many people, and racial inequalities remain evident in schools and throughout society still today (Gottlieb, 2020; Koretz, 2017).

Further, rather than addressing the "achievement gap" and "socioeconomic mobility," we have seen a focus on developing tools that indicate the existence of these stated outcomes. No investment has been made in the remediation of either within society—primarily because these issues are beyond the school and grounded in societal inequity and injustice (Biesta, 2009; Darling-Hammond, 2010; Giroux, 2012; Kumashiro, 2009, 2012; Parkison, 2015; Saltman, 2012). And, despite the stated goal of improving America's standing in the world, the United States' overall standing in the world has diminished since the enactment of NCLB (Darling-Hammond, 2010; Ravitch, 2010) and *Race to the Top* (Ravitch, 2013; Tanner, 2013). As Gottlieb (2020) put it

> The failures of accountability via high stakes testing have illuminated the *inherent* complexity of the educational endeavor itself, such that clearing away what we mistook for an unruly tangle of underbrush did actual damage to the ecosystem we were trying to perfect. (p. 35)

We explore this metaphor of school as an ecosystem in the following section to further illuminate how the AIC has damaged schools.

Problems with Standardizing Everything

As Knoester and Parkison (2017) discuss, in his landmark book, *Seeing Like a State* (1998), James C. Scott examined in detail a broad range of attempts by various states to standardize a particular aspect of governance. They did so to provide new services to large populations and to create efficiencies, and in many cases, these processes worked out well. At other times, however, the processes of standardization led to disaster. Rachel Carson's 1962 seminal work *Silent Spring* also offers a stark example of the impact of standardization and the mechanisms used to impose it. In her intensive study of insecticides, she highlights the detrimental impact of monoculture agriculture and the indiscriminate use of chemical insect sterilization:

> The most flagrant abuses go unchecked in both state and federal agencies. It is not my contention that chemical insecticides must never be used. I do contend that we have put poisonous and biologically potent chemicals indiscriminately into the hands of persons largely or wholly ignorant of their potentials for harm. We have subjected enormous numbers of people to contact with these poisons, without their consent and often without their knowledge. If the Bill of Rights contains no guarantee that a citizen shall be secure against lethal poisons distributed either by private individuals

or by public officials, it is surely only because our forefathers, despite their considerable wisdom and foresight, could conceive of no such problem. (p. 15)

The similarities to the educational ecosystem and the agricultural ecosystem are striking; hence, we utilize an ecological framework as part of our analysis to demonstrate the interconnected relationship of testing and education.

The manipulation of the ecology anchors all stakeholders within a system. Students, teachers, schools, districts, and states become "legible" and "more amenable" to the state apparatus. This leaves us open to significant surveillance and symbolic violence. Scott demonstrates these devastating effects by detailing dozens of examples where techniques of standardization did not work well due to changing populations or to misunderstood complexities in the population or the environment. The most obvious example was that of a map. Maps are necessarily simplified renderings of complex terrain. They are simplified so those using them can more easily understand the world. However, they inevitably render complexities invisible and make normative the political priorities of the mapmaker (placing the United States in the center of the map, for example, while cutting or disfiguring "less important" regions). In another example, Scott described the attempt of early modern German policymakers to harvest the most productive forestry product, the Norway spruce, at the most constant high-volume possible. They planted row upon row of trees at an exact distance from one another to best enable their harvest and cut out any underbrush that might inhibit the process. Although the first generation of these trees provided a strong crop, the managers overlooked the meaningful symbiotic relationships between trees and other living organisms and nutrients in the soil. Almost the entire second crop of trees died from an outbreak of a variety of problems. Since they were spread out, they were more vulnerable to storm feelings; various pests that favored the species, rapidly spread throughout the monocrop, and the soil became depleted of nutrients necessary to nourish the Norway spruce. An ecological view of complex systems like forest biomes could have prevented this loss (Knoester & Parkison, 2017). Bringing simplistic institutional and linear paradigms to bear on complex ecologies brackets consideration of interaction, inter-relation, and complexity that are necessary to understand and work within ecological systems.

The damage caused by treating living things with simplistic and linear standardized techniques can range in severity from minor hardships to the cruelest treatment of human beings imaginable (Carson, 1962, 2002). Scott (1998) argued:

The modern state, through its officials, attempts with varying success to *create a terrain* [emphasis added] and a population with precisely those standardized characteristics that will be easiest to monitor, count, assess, and manage. The utopian, immanent, and continually frustrated goal of the modern state is to reduce the chaotic, disorderly, constantly changing social reality beneath it to something more closely resembling the administrative grid of its observations (pp. 81–82).

We can successfully overcome problems of scale, but improvements must involve learning from past failures (assuming policymakers are dedicated to improving people's lives, which was not always the case in Scott's examples). Policymakers must use their understanding of complexity, hopefully, learned in one context, to inform understanding of other complex contexts.

The imposition of simplistic institutional and linear paradigms represents this type of transfer but one that does not recognize the appropriately analogous context. For example, what works in business and manufacturing does not necessarily transfer to education and schooling. In fact, in 1995, during the inception of the national emphasis in education on content standards and testing, Elliot Eisner (1995) questioned the value of standards applied to educational settings and how such standards should be derived. He stated,

> Beyond the details of the classroom, there are more general questions having to do with the bases on which educational standards are formulated. Should educational standards be derived from the average level of performance of students in a school, in a school district, in a state, in a nation, in the world? How much talk have we heard of 'world-class' standards? (p. 763)

Eisner's comments are particularly interesting against the backdrop of the AIC. To test students, we need to argue at least that the process should be appropriate and fair. This question of what is appropriate and fair, however, is defined through a narrow understanding of what counts as relevant to all students in the process of educating them.

Further, the process is biased toward those with the power to make decisions that impact all students; too often, those decisions continue to benefit those with more access and opportunity than those who are lacking them. Eisner (1995) challenges the notion of standards from this perspective as well:

> If national policy dictates that there will be uniform national standards for student performance, will there also be uniform national standards for the resources available to schools? To teachers? To administrators? Will the differences in performance between students living in well-heeled, upper-class suburbs and those living on the cusp of poverty in the nation's inner cities demonstrate the existing inequities in American education? Will they not merely confirm what we already know? (p. 764)

And Over 25 years later, after the publication of these words, the answer remains NO! Since 1995, the movement to standardize education has exponentially increased, culminating with the publication and dissemination of the Common Core State Standards (CCSS) and each school-age student being required to take a multitude of benchmark and other high-stakes standardized tests throughout the school year. Yet, schools are more segregated by race today than they were after the *Brown v. Board* decision in 1954 (Rosiek & Kinslow, 2015; Strauss, 2013). Furthermore, as mentioned earlier, the expansive testing regime is the anchor that grounds our current standardized system of education and perpetuates a system of inequity and inequality.

Tethering Education to Testing

A myriad of scholars has attested to the continuous increase and impact of corporations on the education system, including dominating the discourse on the purpose of education, what should be included in the curriculum, how we should prepare teachers, etc. (Ravitch, 2020; Saltman, 2017; Tenam-Zemach & Flynn, 2011, 2015). Their arguments exemplify how all other aspects of education are tethered, that is anchored, to assessment. Knoester and Au (2017) describe "high-stakes, standardized testing as the fulcrum upon which education reforms pivot, and as a tool for racializing decisions about children, schools, and communities" (p. 6). In their telling, "fulcrum" is the operative metaphor. This is to picture education reform as moveable by certain levers, which turn upon the fulcrum of achievement data generated by these standardized assessments. However, we take this notion of high-stakes testing and assessments a step further. Instead of thinking of the testing apparatus as constructing a basis upon which reforms turn, we conceptualize the Assessment Industrial Complex as an anchor, which emphasizes how standardized testing restricts the possibilities of changing and evaluating public education, namely by tethering such possibilities to the data generated by these assessments. Such data has become the primary determinant of society's interpretation and definition of "what it means to say a school is doing well" (Eisner, 2001, p. 367) and the primary language in which we can envision the purposes of education.

Thus, we frame the theoretical perspective of our critique on Eisner's ecology of school improvement (1988). As schools aim to do well or make improvements, ecological interactions occur across intentional, structural, curricular, pedagogical, and evaluative dimensions. Through a relationship of interdependence, as one dimension is affected, such as the evaluative dimension through the use of high-stakes assessments, the other dimensions are also affected (Eisner, 1988). Testing provides the "data" required for making all other educational decisions. Those decisions are justified causing an imbalance in the ecology of schooling; when one dimension, let alone one aspect of one dimension like testing, dominates all other ecological dimensions, an imbalance results. Education and educational achievement are based on perception. A variety of processes, conditions, and cultural interpretations yield a variety of understandings of what it means to say a school is doing well (Eisner, 2001). Since Eisner first described this framework, the influence of the AIC has grown and increasingly has dominated these ecological interactions. For example, Conn (2016) found that when the state of Colorado began evaluating teachers based on student "growth," which was determined through standardized assessments, the evaluative dimension controlled the other dimensions. Teachers' intentions, the way they taught, their curriculum design, and the structure of the school day were all predicated on the demands of high-stakes testing.

Consequently, high-stakes testing represents an anchor point within education today. The development of curriculum, lesson plans, formative assessments, and government education policy revolves around the expectations of high-stakes, standardized testing. Whether considered from the vantage point of college and career readiness or disciplinary content knowledge, high-stakes, standardized testing provides content that directs schooling if not education. How we understand this testing assemblage says a great deal about how we relate to and embody education. What occurs in school and individual classrooms is shaped by the relationship we form with our students and the testing regime to which we are subject. The stated intention is that high-stakes tests are meant to help districts, schools, and teachers set goals for what children should know and be able to do as a result of instruction. High-stakes tests, however, do not stand alone; they require implementation through pedagogical strategies in heterogeneous classrooms. Quality implementation of standards requires aligning new curriculum and assessments and the provision of sufficient resources and support for students and teachers.

AIC as Anchor

We argue that the AIC now anchors school ecologies throughout the U.S. Anchors hold things in place—The AIC is an anchor because it grounds all the elements of Eisner's ecology in place; they are all related, and interrelated, and mutually dependent, but the existence of the AIC, precisely by functioning as an anchor, distorts this ecological inter-relationality. No longer are they mutually dependent, answerable as themselves to each of the other elements. They all simply depend on the AICs directives. They do not affect one another; the AIC simply determines their content. Most importantly, perhaps, is that none of the other elements is allowed to affect the AICs priorities; hence, where the AIC is concerned, there is no mutuality in the relation. That is like an anchor. A ship may ordinarily sail, but an anchor prevents its natural motion, and the ship's tendency to sail does not change anything for the anchor; it does not affect it.

In this context, ecologies refer to mutual interactions of five dimensions evident in schools: intentions (both teacher and students), structure (of the classroom and the time and space that it operates within) curriculum (what is taught and not taught), pedagogy (teaching), and evaluation (includes formal and informal judgments on learning; Eisner, 1988). Further, Eisner regarded a focus on assessment as a degraded version of evaluation, one of the elements of schooling's ecology, no more or less. The way an anchor holds something in place that would otherwise move in accordance with natural forces, suggest that this anchoring interrupts the force of natural relationships among schooling elements. Eisner (1988) argues that if one of the five dimensions is impacted, this affects the other dimensions. For example, if a new reading curriculum is adopted in a third-grade classroom, this can affect how long reading is scheduled for (structure) and how reading is taught (pedagogy). A new reading curriculum may also change the way we think about assessing reading and monitoring students' progress (evaluations). We have chosen an anchor metaphor for the AIC because the majority of educational outcomes and expectations are tethered to all forms of testing and the data these assessments produce. These outcomes and expectations have been dictated by a market-driven ideology that has limited society's perception of "what it means to say a school is doing well."

It is particularly troublesome that we now anchor our education system and all forms of school improvement to student testing data. Proponents of the AIC claim the data from tests reveal what students do and do not know and should or should not be able to do; they define this by the content standards each state adopts (currently, 41 of the 50 states in the U.S. have adopted the Common Core State Standards). They also argue that the data reflects and aligns with the values and purposes of education (again, the adopted content standards being utilized exemplify this as well). However, this rhetorical argument is inherently false. While testing data can reveal particular qualities or understandings, they conceal other expressions of learning that are rarely included on standardized assessments (Au, 2011; Conn, 2016; Eisner, 2001). As Eisner (1995) informs his readers:

> The more important work…makes it possible for students to think imaginatively about problems that matter to them, tasks that give them the opportunity to affix their own personal signature to their work, occasions to explore ideas and questions that have no correct answers, and projects in which they can reason and express their own ideas. (p. 764)

In addition to concealing or eschewing positive outcomes, standardized assessments conceal systemic issues, in particular racial and classist problems. When it serves their interests, proponents utilize the data to make the learning conditions appear better than they are (Koretz, 2017), creating an illusion that the AIC is helping, when, in fact, educational circumstances are growing worse, especially for marginalized students (Knoester & Au, 2017).

During the coronavirus epidemic, for example, states may have relaxed annual high-stakes standardized testing requirements; nevertheless, they continue to use the rhetoric of the AIC to make it clear that tested subjects, such as reading and math, matter most, and that equity would be achieved through holding school districts, schools, teachers and counselors accountable for student academic achievement. One specific instance of this is The North Dakota Department of Public Instruction's (2020) release of their District Distance Learning Expectations document. This document outlined the district requirements for their submission of their plan to address teaching online. The "intent" of the state, according to the document, is "To educate and graduate the students of North Dakota through the end of the academic year while maintaining the health and safety of students, staff, and community" (paragraph 2). The next paragraph focuses on equity as a "critical consideration," of the expectations set forth for districts. The state offers three options regarding the instruction of content: exposure to content, supplemental content, and full continuation. However, "only a plan that outlines a full continuation of services will be considered as replacing instructional time" (paragraph 8). While both exposure and supplemental content limit the expectations on assessment or evaluation of work, full continuation of content must include "assessment and evaluation of work" and "measurable student progress is expected" (paragraph 11). Thus, the only distant education plan that is acceptable, during, by the way, the worst pandemic in America's history, is one that includes testing that measures students' academic progress. Never mind that districts were only given four days to develop and submit these plans or that teachers in the state of ND may lack any experience or understanding of how to educate their students at a distance. What matters is that the outcomes are measurable, as determined by the state.

Our Concerns About the AIC

Through critical analysis of the AIC, we argue that the AIC usurps dialogue while reinforcing historical hierarchies of control and symbolic violence. Not only does the AIC anchor educational policy to testing, but it enables corporate and political failures to beget more opportunities for corporate and political profit. This dynamic leaves community schools in omnishambles, ripe for Edreformers [our nomenclature for education reformers] to further capitalize on both real and manufactured failures. After almost four decades of bi-partisan, neoliberal education policy, we have a system that rewards corporations for perceived deficiencies with more opportunities to privatize education (Apple, 2006). For example, the recent 2019 NAEP report reveals that reading scores have dropped across the country, and education reformers are already using this as a rationale for more privatization (Green & Goldstein, 2019). According to DeVos, the NAEP results, "must be America's wake up call" (paragraph 4), and she concluded, "we can neither excuse them away nor simply throw more money at the problem" (paragraph 5). This rhetoric means DeVos and other Edreformers will, of course, use the opportunity to justify more neoliberal policies in the name of "saving the children." And these policies will reinforce the anchor of testing and further distort school ecologies. As described above, curriculum, pedagogy, and virtually all other educational decisions will be further tied to tests and testing preparation. Undoubtedly, left unchallenged, these policies will result in more standardized tests and standardized curriculum designed to teach what will be on the standardized tests. Ladson-Billings (2014), Knoester and Au (2017), Royal and Gibson (2017), Tenam-Zemach and Flynn (2015), Weiner (2015), and others argue that standardized curricula and assessments are hierarchical by nature and reinforce existing power structures. Thus, the continuation of these policies especially is concerning because it will continue a cycle of symbolic violence toward students and their families.

The AIC as Subjects of Intention

In many cases, we are tempted to approach high-stakes testing and the AIC as objects of inquiry and implementation and not as *subjects of intention* in dialogue. Recognizing both standardized tests and the AIC as *subjects of intention* leads to engaging with them as subjects that are a powerful presence with agency as goal-directed phenomena open to dialogue. This recognition is significantly different from approaching high-stakes tests and the AIC as static objects of study. It is common to see high-stakes tests as an object of study or as a set of restraining requirements for the development of curricula, discrete lesson plans, and formative assessment instruments. The consequence of not considering high-stakes tests as subjects of intention, defined by our purpose concerning them, is profound. We are approaching high-stakes tests from an orientation that appreciates their role as contextual actors that have the potential to transform education, schooling, the development of curriculum, and classroom instructional practices. If we maintain a constraining separation between the products or objects of high-stakes tests (test preparation materials, curriculum pacing guides, formative assessment products, and the test scores), and our purpose in creating curricula and educative experiences within a schooling context, then the culture will develop immanently, in ways which are unpredictable (Hirschkop, 1989).

Students who lack the opportunity to engage in meaningful educational experiences fail to understand their role in a democracy, to develop an understanding of the self, or the connection between their education and their potential future. Students, captured by schooling within the AIC paradigm, become disconnected automatons who do not value the educational experiences that emerge through the cracks and gaps in the AIC system; they fail to understand their potential role in society, and find little value in what their school experiences have to offer (Samuels & Samuels, 2019). Consequently, high-stakes testing and this type of evaluation environment constitute an act of psychological and moral violence toward human dignity; as such, we believe it is imperative to disrupt the AIC. Finally, as educators committed to a social justice orientation in our education system, we recognize that our interrogation of high-stakes tests and the AIC develops a mode of discourse that engages and disrupts the normative, value-laden connection between the lessons, curriculum, and assessments, and the AIC as intentional subjects. We also acknowledge that not all forms of assessments are inherently damaging or ominous. One of our primary contentions is that how assessments are utilized throughout the entire educational system supports a narrative of legitimacy that is neither valid nor legitimate. We also recognize that there are no simple or quick solutions to the issues with standardized testing. Its ubiquity and roots, as we argue throughout this book, are firmly planted in educational systems throughout this country and the world at large (NACAC, 2020). Nevertheless, we are firmly committed to unraveling the AIC to demonstrate that it is our responsibility as a nation to understand the damage it has done and continues to do to our students, teachers, and society.

References

Apple, M. (2006). *Educating the "right" way: Markets, standards, God, and inequality* (2nd ed.). Routledge.

Au, W. (2007). High-stakes testing and curricular control: A qualitative metasynthesis. *Educational Researcher, 36*(5), 258–267.

Au, W. (2011). Teaching under the new Taylorism: High--stakes testing and the standardization of the 21st century curriculum. *Journal of Curriculum Studies, 43*(1), 25–45.

Biesta, G. J. (2009). Good education in an age of measurement: On the need to reconnect with the question of purpose in education. *Educational Assessment. Evaluation and Accountability, 21,* 33–46. 10.1007/s11092-008-9064-9

Bourdieu, P. (1979). Symbolic power. *Critique of Anthropology, 4,* 77–85.

Carson, R. (1962). *Silent spring.* Boston, MA: Houghton Mifflin Company.

Carson, R. (2002). *Silent spring.* (40th Anniversary ed.). Boston, MA: Houghton Mifflin Company.

Chomsky, N. (1999). *Profit over people: Neoliberalism and global order.* New York, NY: Seven Stories Press.

Chomsky, N. (2017). *Noam Chomsky: Neoliberalism is destroying our democracy [Interview by C. Lydon, 2017, June 2). The Nation.* Retrieved from https://chomsky.info/06022017/.

Conn, D. R. (2016). What are we doing to kids here? *Curriculum and Teaching Dialogue, 18*(1-2), 25–40.

Darling-Hammond, L. (2006). Assessing teacher education: The usefulness of multiple measures for assessing program outcomes. *Journal of Teacher Education, 57*(2), 120–138.

Darling-Hammond, L. (2010). *The flat world and education: How America's commitment to equity will determine our future.* New York, NY: Teachers College Press.

Dean, C., Hubbell, E., Pitler, H., & Stone, B. (2012). *Classroom instruction that works: Research-based strategies for increasing student achievement.* Boston, MA: Pearson Teacher Education/Association for Supervision and Curriculum Development.

Deleuze, G., & Guattari, F. (1987). *A thousand plateaus: Capitalism and schizophrenia* (B. Massumi Trans.). Minneapolis: University of Minnesota Press.

Eisenhower, D. D. (1961). *Farewell address.* Dwight D. Eisenhower Presidential Library, Museum and Boyhood Home. Retrieved from https://www.eisenhowerlibrary.gov/sites/default/files/research/online-documents/farewell-address/reading-copy.pdf.

Eisner, E. W. (1988). The ecology of school improvement. *Educational Leadership, 45*(5), 24–29.

Eisner, E. W. (1995). Standards for American schools: Help or hindrance? *Phi Delta Kappan, 76*(10), 758–764.

Eisner, E. W. (2001). What does it mean to say a school is doing well? *Phi Delta Kappan, 82*(5), 367–372.

Freire, P. (1972). *Cultural action for freedom*. London, UK: Penguin Books.

Gaventa, J. (1980). *Power and powerlessness: Quiescence and rebellion in an Appalachian valley*. Urbana: University of Illinois Press.

Giroux, H. A. (2012). *Education and the crisis of public values: Challenging the assault on teachers, students, and public education*. New York, NY: Peter Lang.

Goodman, S. (2018). *It's not about grit: Trauma, inequity, and the power of transformative teaching*. Goodman, NY: Teachers College Press.

Gottlieb, D. (2020). *A democratic theory of educational accountability*. London, UK: Routledge.

Green, E. L., & Goldstein, D. (2019, October 30). Reading scores on national exam decline in half the states. *The New York Times*. Retrieved from https://www.nytimes.com/2019/10/30/us/reading-scores-national-exam.html.

Green, E. L., & Goldstein, D. (2019, December). Reading scores on national exam decline in half the states. *The New York Times*. Retrieved from https://www.nytimes.com/2019/10/30/us/reading-scores-national-exam.html.

Hargreaves, A., & Fullan, M. (2012). *Professional capital: Transforming teaching in every school*. New York, NY: Teachers College Press.

Hart, R., Casserly, M., Uzzell, R., Palacios, M., Corcoran, A., & Spurgeon, L. (2015). *Student testing in America's great city schools: An inventory and preliminary analysis [White paper]*. Council of the Great City Schools. Retrieved from https://www.cgcs.org/cms/lib/DC00001581/Centricity/Domain/87/Testing%20Report.pdf.

Hartung, W. D. (2010). *Prophets of war: Lockheed Martin and the making of the military-industrial complex*. New York, NY: Nation Books.

Hirschkop, K. (1989). Introduction: Bakhtin and cultural theory. In K. Hirschkop & D. Shepherd (Eds.), *Bahktin and cultural theory* (pp. 1–38). Manchester, UK: Manchester University Press.

Knoester, M., & Au, W. (2017). Standardized testing and school segregation: Like tinder for fire? *Race Ethnicity and Education, 20*(1), 1–14.

Knoester, M., & Parkison, P. (2017). Seeing like a state: How education policy misreads what is important in schools. *Education Studies, 53*(3), 247–262.

Koretz, D. (2017). *The testing charade: Pretending to make schools better*. Chicago, IL: University of Chicago Press.

Kraska, P. B. (2007). Militarization and policing—Its relevance to 21st century police. *Policing: A Journal of Policy and Practice, 1*(4), 501–513.

Kumashiro, K. (2009). *Against common sense: Teaching and learning toward social justice*. (Rev. ed.). London, UK: Routledge.

Kumashiro, K. K. (2012). *Bad teacher! How blaming teachers distorts the bigger picture*. New York, NY: Teachers College Press.

Ladner, M., & Myslinski, D. (2013). *Report card on American education: Ranking state K-12 performance, progress, and reform*. Washington, DC: American Legislative Exchange Council.

Ladson-Billings, G. (2014). Culturally relevant pedagogy 2.0: Aka the remix. *Harvard Educational Review, 84*(1), 74–84.

Ledbetter, J. (2011). *Unwarranted influence: Dwight D. Eisenhower and the military industrial complex*. London, UK: Yale University Press.

National Association for College Admission Counseling. (2020). *Access to higher education: The role of standardized Testing in the time of COVID-19 And beyond Guidance for colleges.* Retrieved from https://www.nacacnet.org/globalassets/documents/knowledge-center/nacac_testingtaskforcereport.pdf.

Levine, A. (2010). Teacher education must respond to changes in America. *Kappan, 92*(2), 19–24.

Martinez, E., & Garcia, A. (1997, January 1). What is neo-liberalism? A brief definition. *CorpWatch.* Retrieved from https://corpwatch.org/article/what-neoliberalism.

McDonald, M., Kazemi, E., & Schneider-Kavanagh, S. (2013). Core practices and pedagogies of teacher education: A call for a common language and collective activity. *Journal of Teacher Education, 64*(5), 378–386.

North Dakota Department of Public Instruction. (2020). *District distance learning expectations.* Retrieved from https://www.nd.gov/dpi/sites/www/files/documents/Covid19/Distance%20Learning%20(FINAL).pdf.

Parkison, P. (2015). Catharsis in education: Rationalizing and reconciling. *Journal of Curriculum and Teaching Dialogue, 17*(2), 121–136.

Phi Delta Kappan. (2017). *Why school? The 48th annual PDK poll of the public's attitudes toward the public schools.* Retrieved from https://pdkpoll.org/wpcontent/uploads/2020/05/pdkpoll48_2016.pdf.

Picciano, A. G. (1994). Technology and the evolving educational-industrial complex. *Computers in the Schools, 11*(2), 85–102.

Ravitch, D. (2001). *Left back: A century of battles over school reform.* New York, NY: Simon and Schuster.

Ravitch, D. (2010). *The death and life of the great American school system: How testing and choice are undermining education.* New York, NY: Basic Books.

Ravitch, D. (2013). *Reign of error: The hoax of the privatization movement and the danger to America's public schools.* New York, NY: Vintage.

Ravitch, D. (2020). *Slaying Goliath: The passionate resistance to privatization and the fight to save America's public schools.* New York, NY: Knopf.

Rosiek, J., & Kinslow, K. (2015). *Resegregation as curriculum: The meaning of the new racial segregation in U.S. public schools.* London, UK: Routledge.

Royal, C., & Gibson, S. (2017). They schools: Culturally relevant pedagogy under siege. *Teachers College Record, 119*(1), 1–25.

Saltman, K. J. (2012). *The failure of corporate school reform.* Boulder, CO: Paradigm Publishers.

Saltman, K. J. (2017). *Scripted Bodies: Corporate power, smart technologies, and the undoing of public education.* London, UK: Routledge.

Saltman, K. J. (2018). *The politics of education: A critical introduction.* London, UK: Routledge.

Samuels, G. & Samuels, A. (Eds.). (2019). *Democracy at a crossroads: Reconceptualizing sociopolitical issues in schools and society.* Charlotte, NC: Information Age Publishing, Inc.

Scott, J. C. (1998). *Seeing like a state: How certain schemes to improve the human condition have failed.* London, UK: Yale University Press.

Spring, J., & Picciano, A. G. (2013). *The great American education-industrial complex: Ideology, technology, and profit.* London, UK: Routledge.

Strauss, V. (2013, February 9). Global education market reaches $4.4 trillion—and is growing. *The Washington Post.* Retrieved from https://www.washingtonpost.com/news/answer-sheet/wp/2013/02/09/global-education-market-reaches-4-4-trillion-and-is-growing/?utm_term=.be48be2f99a3.

Strauss, V. (2013, February 9). Report: Public schools more segregated now than 40 years ago. *The Washington Post*. Retrieved from https://www.washingtonpost.com/news/answer-sheet/wp/2013/08/29/report-public-schools-more-segregated-now-than-40-years-ago/.

Strauss, V. (2018, June 8). The bottom line on opting out of high-stakes standardized tests. *The Washington Post*. Retrieved from https://www.washingtonpost.com/news/answer-sheet/wp/2018/06/08/the-bottom-line-on-opting-out-of-high-stakes-standardized-tests/.

Strauss, V. (2019, December 31). Arguably the two most appalling stories about the standardized testing obsession of the 2010s. *The Washington Post*. Retrieved from https://www.washingtonpost.com/education/2019/12/31/arguably-two-most-appalling-stories-about-standardized-testing-obsession-s/.

Sudbury, J. (2014). *Global lockdown: Race, gender, and the prison-industrial complex*. London, UK: Routledge.

Tanner, D. (2013). Race to the top and leave the children behind. *Journal of Curriculum Studies, 45*(1), 4–15.

Taylor, A., & Karklis, L. (2016, February 09). *This remarkable chart shows how U.S. defense spending dwarfs the rest of the world*. Retrieved from https://www.washingtonpost.com/news/worldviews/wp/2016/02/09/this-remarkable-chart-shows-how-u-s-defense-spending-dwarfs-the-rest-of-the-world.

Tenam-Zemach, M., & Flynn, J. (2011). America's rise [race] to the top: Our fall from grace. *Curriculum and Teaching Dialogue, 13*(2), 113–124.

Tenam-Zemach, M., & Flynn, J. (Eds.). (2015). *Rubric nation: Critical inquiries into the impacts of rubrics on education*. Charlotte, NC: Information Age Publications.

The National Commission on Excellence in Education. (1983, April). *A nation at risk: The imperative for educational reform*. Retrieved from https://edreform.com/wp-content/uploads/2013/02/A_Nation_At_Risk_1983.pdf.

Thomas, J. Y., & Brady, K. P. (2005). Chapter 3: The elementary and secondary education Act at 40: Equity, accountability, and the evolving federal role in public education. *Review of Research in Education, 29*(1), 51–67.

Venugopal, R. (2015). Neoliberalism as concept. *Economy and Society, 44*(2), 165–187.

Wagner, T. (2008). *The global achievement gap*. New York, NY: Basic Books.

Weiner, E. J. (2015). *Deschooling the imagination: Critical thought as social practice*. London, UK: Routledge.

Wiggins, G., & McTighe, J. (2005). *Understanding by design* (2nd ed.). Alexandria, VA: Association for Supervision and Curriculum Development ASCD.

Zhao, Y. (2018). *What works may hurt—Side effects in education*. New York, NY: Teachers College Press.

2

TESTING AND SOCIETY

How We Got to Where We Are

Origins of Testing in the United States

Since the days of Horace Mann, and later iterations of the Common School era, testing has been widely accepted as a valid approach to measure students' learning: what they know and are able to do as a result of instruction. Mann was a prominent member of the Whig Party, Secretary of the Massachusetts State Board of Education, and later served in the U.S. House of Representatives. Mann is mainly known for his support of universal education, but he has another long-lasting legacy in the American education system—testing. Reese (2013) provides a thorough history detailing the rise of testing in the United States, illuminating how testing, even in its early conception, was used as a political tool to control educators. Before the administration of paper-and-pencil tests, common schools were evaluated through public oral examinations, where students would perform and recite what they had learned before the broader community. Through this practice, public impressions essentially determined the worth of a school and assessed the degree to which students were learning. Though public examinations were popular, Mann and his political allies argued that New England schools were declining in quality. Teachers and students often focused on what would be performed in the expositions while neglecting content and skills that were not performed. Thus, communities lacked an objective way of ensuring schools were adequately teaching students what they needed to know. Though it took many resources and political will for Mann and his allies to effectively replace public examinations with written ones, the introduction of tests into the American education system created the beginning of a paradigm shift in education. Tests reframed what should be taught, what counted as learning, and they were taken individually rather than performed communally. This framework, where learning is thought to be a competition whose scores determine who are the winners and losers, was reinforced by capitalistic notions of individuality and perceptions of merit. Though the implications of this framework would play out over time, the shift from the community to the individual was a dramatic shift from community examinations—where students, teachers, and headmasters were in it together to some degree—to a world where students, teachers, and entire schools were competing against one another. Additionally, Mann and his allies proved testing could be used as a political tool by sharing the results of the tests with local newspapers and political circles to demonstrate that the headmasters were too narrowly focused on discipline and not enough on academic content. Tests were adopted across New England; Mann and his allies used test results as a way to shame headmasters and rhetorically control the conversation about what counted for learning (Peterson, 2010; Reese, 2013; Rothman; 2001).

This use of power within education is an example of how dominant groups control a political situation through the defining of legitimacy. In the case of the use of testing to control education, their identification with legitimacy involved specifying the means through which power influences, shapes, or determines conceptions of the necessities, possibilities, and strategies of challenge within situations of latent conflict. Mann and his allies were able to control the terms of the dialogue while the headmasters were quiescent. It is essential to recognize how information is communicated, both what is communicated and how it is done. It involves focusing on how social legitimations are developed around the dominant and instilled as beliefs or roles in the dominated. It involves locating the power processes behind the social construction of meanings and patterns (Gaventa, 1980; Mueller, 1972).

Hence, for Mann, not only did testing provide an opportunity rhetorically to shift what it means to learn, but it was also, and still is, used as a political apparatus. For example, in the 1850s, less than a decade after written testing emerged in New England common schools, literacy tests were used as a way to deny adult citizens access to voting. After ratification of the 15th Amendment to the U.S. Constitution in 1868, literacy tests, primarily, were used to deny former slaves and other people of color the right to vote (Filer, Kenny, & Morton, 1991). This occurred most predominantly in Southern states until the Civil Rights Act of 1964 and the Voting Rights Act of 1965, which made this practice illegal (Cascio & Washington, 2013). Although literacy tests are no longer used to deny certain groups access to the ballot, tests are still used as gatekeepers for opportunity and access.

Testing as the Gatekeeper

By the end of the 19th century, testing had become quite common and mainstream across the United States, and public evaluations were passé (Reese, 2013). Testing was used to determine who could graduate and otherwise fully participate in society. Testing became a gatekeeper and, with that, a ubiquitous construct within the American education system. Tests were and still are used as a means to ensure a person is qualified for a professional or academic position. Late 19th and early 20th century schools utilized what was known as "Common Exams" to determine whether the graduating eighth graders should attend high school. For example, eighth-grade students from one-room schoolhouses in Bullitt County Kentucky came together at the county courthouse once or twice a year to take a Common Exam, which included spelling, arithmetic, grammar, geography, physiology, civil government, and history. Though these examinations were different from the public examinations of the common schools' era and the high-stakes environment of modern times, there was still plenty of public attention and implied pressure. According to the Bullitt County History (n.d.):

> The local newspaper urged students to do well, even urging seventh graders that it was not too early to start preparing. Some scholarships were provided to those who passed to go on to high school, which was also a big deal back then. In those days, high school was sometimes another county away and a rare thing for many farm children to be able to otherwise attend.
>
> *(paragraph 3)*

In addition to using tests as a way to determine whether eighth graders were fit for high school, tests were also used by schools to measure intelligence. Books like *Mental Tests for School Use* by Charles E. Holley (1920) argued for the use of intelligence tests as a way to measure the extent to which teachers should invest their time and energy into helping individual students that struggled in school. Holley noted, "It is apparent that the movement to measure intelligence by means of group tests is well under way" (p. 5). This development added a layer to testing as a form of gatekeeping. Instead of measuring who should be allowed in (or kept out) based on merit, intelligence tests implied biological limitations and, as we discuss in the next section, reinforced systemic inequalities, including White supremacy. As Stovall (2016) explains, "White supremacy is an ideological concept that holds the media-influenced and government-sponsored values of American White, Western European descended-heterosexual Christian male as normative" (p. 5). Tests provided a construct for the dominant culture to control the narrative for what counts for beauty and intelligence.

Testing for Eugenics

Stoskopf (2002), Au (2009), Knoester and Au (2017), Kendi (2016), and others have recounted that early intelligence tests, especially the IQ test, have roots in the eugenics movement. Though the concept of breeding humans for selective genetic qualities has been around for centuries, the term "eugenics" specifically refers to a movement, popularized in the United Kingdom, that spread across

Europe as well as North America, based on Darwin's theory of natural selection (Galton, 1904). Regarding testing, Alfred Binet and Theophi Simon developed an intelligence test in 1905, the Binet-Simon Scale. Lewis Terman and his colleagues at Stanford University modified this concept and eventually developed the Stanford-Binet Intelligence Scale, which became known as the "intelligence quotient" or IQ (Roid & Pomplun, 2012; Shanklin, 1994). The "science" behind the eugenics movement was eventually used as a rationale for policies from Ernst Rüdin, Adolph Hitler, and other prominent Nazis.

Eugenics principles are built on racist ideas, and those ideas eventually led to policies and laws that discriminated against a wide range of people. According to the Holocaust Encyclopedia (n.d.),

> In formulating their ideology of race, Hitler and the Nazis drew upon the ideas of the German social Darwinists of the late 19th century. Like the social Darwinists before them, the Nazis believed that human beings could be classified collectively as "races," with each race bearing distinctive characteristics that had been passed on genetically since the first appearance of humans in prehistoric times. These inherited characteristics related not only to outward appearance and physical structure, but also shaped internal mental life, ways of thinking, creative and organizational abilities, intelligence, taste and appreciation of culture, physical strength, and military prowess.
>
> *(paragraph 6)*

Consequently, these beliefs eventually became laws and policies that targeted a wide range of historically marginalized groups: Jews, Roma (Gypsies), Poles, Soviet prisoners of war, Afro-Germans, people with disabilities, Jehovah's Witnesses, homosexuals, intellectuals, non-conformists, radicals and all other political dissidents. As is detailed in William Shirer's *The Rise and Fall of the Third Reich,* eugenics provides a surface layer understanding of Nazi race theory and ideas. The more profound significance, and one that has equally foundational implications for testing's role within education, is ontological:

> …[W]ith this mention of the preservation of the species and of the race in *Mein Kampf* we come to the second principle of consideration: Hitler's *Weltanschauung*, his view of life,…Like Darwin but also like a whole array of German philosophers, historians, kings, generals and statesmen, Hitler saw life as an eternal struggle and the world as a jungle where the fittest survived and the strongest ruled—a "world where one creature feeds on the other and where the death of the weaker implies the life of the stronger."
>
> *(Shirer, 1960, p. 86)*

While the oppressive and marginalizing impact of testing is essential to problematize, it is equally significant to acknowledge how testing serves to legitimate claims of superiority and high-achievement. Testing builds from the assumption that life is a competitive process with winners and losers.

Although the eugenics movement did not lead to widespread Nazism in the United States, it was relatively mainstream throughout the progressive period. Influential voices from all sectors of society supported eugenics, including Theodore Roosevelt, Oliver Wendell Holmes Jr., Alexander Graham Bell, W.E.B. Du Bois, and Margerret Sanger (Dowbiggin, 1997; Lombardo, 2011; Winfield, 2007). Despite widespread acceptance at the time, the logic behind the eugenics movement was based on assumptions of the scientists, which were constructed in a world filled with systemic racism and White supremacy. As Gould (1994) put it:

> In assessing the impact of science upon 18th and 19th-century views of race, we must recognize the cultural milieu or a society whose leaders and intellectuals did not doubt the propriety or racial-with ranking Indians below whites and blacks below everyone else. (p. 63)

Knoester and Au (2017) provide several examples of this dynamic, including the Alpha and Beta Army standardized tests used to assess the intelligence of incoming army recruits during World War I. According to the Alpha and Beta, people with lighter complexions of skin were more intelligent than people with darker complexions, and people of African descent were least intelligent (Giordano, 2005). Additionally, it is essential to recognize the historical contexts of so-called "intelligence" and "aptitude" tests. For example, the military rethought their approach to testing in the late 1960s to account for racial and gender-based biases; nonetheless, they have a long history of rewarding dominant culture and power structures (Valentine, 1977). The Armed Services Vocational Aptitude Battery (ASVAB), for example, is based heavily on the Armed Forces Qualification Test (AFQT). Each branch of the military has its version of the AFQT. Connor and Vargyas (1992), Roberts and Skinner (1996), Rodgers and Spriggs (1996), Valentine (1977), and a long list of others, have found objective, historical proof of racial and gender bias on the AFQT.

Not only was there a history of racial and gender bias on the AFQT, but the data was also manipulated. A well-known example is when Herrnstein and Murray (1994) used results from the AFQT to argue that intelligence was the most contributing factor to achievement rather than other environmental factors beyond the individual's control, such as their socioeconomic status. Paradoxically, they contended that environment, along with genetics, did indeed determine a person's financial income, job performance, birth out of wedlock, and criminality. Their controversial text, *The Bell Curve*, was met with a myriad of criticism for the seemingly primary emphasis that was placed on genetics (Chomsky, 1995; Gould, 1994; Graves, 2001; Heckman, 1995). *The Bell Curve* was intensely criticized for suggesting there are inherent differences in intelligence between the races. Though the text does not explicitly state it, it implies that people of color have inferior genetic intelligence. Graves (2001) referred to *The Bell Curve* as "racist science" (p. 8), arguing the data weakly support the claims made in the text and that the policy recommendations are essentially racist. Although Herrnstein and Murray never actually stated that the racial differences are predominantly genetic, they imply this conclusion with indirect statements. For example, they state, "If tomorrow you knew beyond a shadow of a doubt that all the cognitive differences between races were 100% genetic in origin, nothing of any significance should change" (p. 314). It is also worth noting that Herrnstein and Murray are using the AFQT to measure intelligence, but many have argued that is not what it was designed to measure. Instead, it was designed to measure word knowledge and paragraph comprehension skills that are highly dependent on environmental conditions such as the amount and quality of formal schooling. This example further demonstrates how data can be manipulated to make false claims about genetic causes of differences in racial groups based on tests that are designed to measure skills that are heavily mediated by environmentally mediated privilege (Heckman, 1995).

Likewise, Herrnstein and Murray delete the timed test of numerical operations from the composite AFQT score; however, this subtest is the most accurate predictor of military salary. As there is not a strong correlation with other subsets—and that the best predictor of their salary is weakly correlated with their g factor (a unitary psychometric construct to measure general intelligence)—leaves one to question if their empirical analysis is biased (because they disregard the test with the most predictive certainty). As we demonstrate throughout this book, standardized tests can perpetuate racial inequalities by overemphasizing inherited abilities and deemphasizing the effects of environmental factors such as unequal privilege and systematic racism that perpetuate racial differences. *The Bell Curve* is a poignant example of how inconclusive interpretations of data, data that is assumed (and sometimes argued) to be objective and without bias or manipulation, prop up racism and White supremacy.

The AIC: A Racist Binary

In his recent publication, *How to Be an Antiracist*, Kendi (2019) offers a simple position: one is either racist or antiracist; a person cannot be neutral or claim that they are "not racist." Claiming to be "not racist" does not make you antiracist, and unless a person is striving and fighting (progressive tense is intentional as this is an ongoing process) to ensure that policies, or as Kendi (2019) defines them "written and unwritten laws, rules, procedures, processes, regulations, and guidelines that govern people" (p. 18) are antiracist, any ignorance or acceptance of those policies is inherently racist. Kendi posits the most apparent conclusion about racist ideas: "A racist idea is any idea that suggests one racial group is inferior or superior to another racial group in any way" (p. 20). Regarding testing, for example, one can easily imagine why the entire testing industry is racist. Testing data, and the discourse that collocates with this data, create perceptions about specific groups, typically African-American and LatinX.

Interpretations of testing data implicate these students' levels of proficiency as "inferior" to those of White students, thus elevating (i.e., reinforcing the superiority of) White students in our society. Yet, Edreformers mask these racist constructs with rhetoric like "academic achievement gap" and "standards and accountability." All of these terms are codes used to reinforce and expand racist policies, such as *No Child Left Behind* (U.S. Department of Education, 2002) and *Race to the Top* (U.S. Department of Education, 2009). These policies further marginalize Black and Brown bodies while safeguarding the privileges of those in power, mainly those who are White and affluent. When White liberals claim that they are not racist, but they protect their privilege by supporting policies that maintain their superior position, they are being racist; according to Kendi, the color of the person's skin is irrelevant. Anyone in any form of power, irrespective of their race, can be racist if they uphold and protect policies that create inequality and further inequities. Kendi points out that people from all walks of life can think and do racist things without even realizing it; racist thoughts and actions can eventually lead to racist policies and laws, even when civil rights leaders enact those laws and policies.

One good example of Kendi's (2016) argument is represented by civil rights groups who have defended standardized testing. Kendi (2016) states, "some of the greatest defenders of standardized testing are civil rights leaders, who rely on the testing data in their well-meaning lobbying efforts for greater accountability and resources" (paragraph 13). For Kendi, while these may be well-meaning attempts to close the achievement gap, it perpetuates racist ideas because it creates a debilitating and marginalizing habitus. It locates the power processes behind the racist social construction of meanings and patterns that prompt oppressed people to act and believe in a manner in which they otherwise would not and to the benefit and maintenance of the dominant group. Furthermore, in a raced and racist world, the psychosomatic self necessarily will be racially and racistly constituted. Race is not a veneer lacquered over a nonracial core. It composes the very bodily and physical beings that humans are and the particular ways by which humans engage the world. Like gender and sexism, sexuality and compulsory heterosexuality, disability and bias toward ability, class and class oppression, and other characteristics of contemporary human beings, race and White privilege are constitutive features of human existence and experience as they currently occur. Sometimes habitas is consciously felt, other times not, but in all cases, it helps comprise who and what human beings are.

The habitus of race are simultaneously limiting and enabling. They provide how one can take action in the world, and in so doing, they also foreclose other possible frames of action. Habitus means that a person is not a blank slate, nor is she radically free to transact with the world in any way that she might consciously will. Habitus is that which provides agency for how a person can be impactful, successful, oppressed, or useful in the world. To aptly summarize one scholar's perspective of the effects of racism on our society: "you may not be a hateful and racist person, but you are deeply informed by a hateful and racist society" (D. Stovall, personal communication, May 15, 2020). That hateful and racist society is the habitus that ringfences the possibilities for one's action such that not all modes of engagement are available, but it also is an important means by which a person can act in the world. A blank slate, if an individual or community could exist as one, would not be free, but relatively powerless. Freedom and limitation are not necessarily opposed. Freedom and power are found in and through the constitution of habitus not through its elimination.

As a component of habitus race often functions subconsciously as a predisposition for acting in the world that one does not consciously choose or plan. Because raced predispositions often actively subvert efforts to understand or change them, making themselves inaccessible to conscious inquiry, race often functions unconsciously as well. Both the subconscious and unconscious aspects of habitus can be either limiting or enabling—or both—depending on the particular situation. For example, to be a White person means that one tends to assume that all cultural and social spaces are potentially available for one to inhabit. Instead of acknowledging others' particular interests, needs, and desires, White people who are ontologically expansive tend to recognize only their own needs and desire to occupy space, ignoring how the power provided by White privilege in particular often oppresses others.

Testing, as it has developed from within the context of the politics of education and eugenics, illustrates the double bind of habitus. Tests, and the political economy of test scores and the AIC's hegemony, capture and enframe all of education—not just the education of the oppressed, disempowered, or powerless. While there is privilege within the construct of the test, a person's race, gender, socioeconomic status, and cultural background are advantaged or disadvantaged; all are forced to participate within the narrow confines of the educational system as enframed by testing. As we discuss below, Edreformers and edu-philanthropists are equally subject to capture by the AIC. The rhetoric of test scores is the lens through which education is viewed. Arguments for reform and innovation rely upon the rhetoric generated by the AIC and test scores. Any reform agenda or financial investment in a pet initiative is legitimated with appeal to a rise in test scores and the closing of gaps.

Enframing the AIC

Utilizing Martin Heidegger's thought in the context of enframing ideologies and hegemonic regimes of power is problematic given his history as a Nazi sympathizer and supporter, as revealed in the "Black Notebooks" (Farin & Malpas, 2018; Mitchell & Trawny, 2017). In the "Black Notebooks," a three-volume set of philosophic journals in which Heidegger reveals the depths of his anti-Semitism and adoption of the construct of "world Judaism," we see an example of the type of enframing that this text critiques in the AIC's hegemony. Heidegger grounds his thoughts regarding instrumentality, machinations, and dominating manipulation in a racist construct of oppression. In recognition of the problematic use of Heidegger, we have followed the line of reasoning shared in Jacques Derrida's book "*Of Spirit: Heidegger and the Question*" (Derrida, 1989). Derrida defends Heidegger by showing that the underpinnings of his philosophy—his vocabulary and his network of metaphors—were the same as those of the era's contemporary thinkers. We move forward utilizing Heidegger constructs with an awareness of his problematic positioning and the anti-Semitism that is potentially freighted into the critique of the AIC. We intend to engage with Heidegger's work constructively in awareness of the legacy his thought carries. We do not view Heidegger's Nazism as merely personal or banal, as Hannah Arendt might have argued (Benhabib, 2000; Kristeva, 2001); he is responsible for the origins of his ideas even as we try to reform, reframe, and utilize them.

Current educational narrative is deeply rooted in a technological approach to life that Heidegger (1977) terms *Gestell* or the enframing. Heidegger does not talk of technology as a tool or set of tools, but rather as a way of seeing the world that has, at its heart, a means-end instrumentality. He argues that our whole way of thinking has become technological, colonizing the world with an associated focus on issues such as accountability, standards, competencies, mastery, improvement, and managerialism. For Heidegger, the ethical emerges within the relational condition of care (or what we care about) that accompanies our experiences in the world. This care is contextual, specific to the particular space we inhabit, and it emerges as a consequence of the conceptual frame from which we start. What we pay attention to, the issues and experiences that we choose to respond to, and ways of behaving, speaking, and responding that we make our habits begin within a specific cultural narrative. We care about what we are culturally conditioned to care about—this occurs both consciously and subconsciously through the technologies that enframe our experiences. The conceptual frame that characterizes the AIC hegemony as high-stakes evaluation, grading, and accountability has the dangerous power of technology. What we care about, where we place priorities, enframes the experiences we have available to us. The danger of the co-optation and monopolization of education by the AIC is the foreclosure of heterogeneous and empowering learning that is possible in every school and classroom.

The current pandemic has further exacerbated the reliance on technology to attempt to address educational goals and outcomes. Edtech companies are keenly aware that a door of opportunity has just opened to allow them access to school funding sources that will further increase the presence of technology in students' lives (as well as their profit margins). Under the guise of "personalized learning," edtech supporters, who have long clamored that traditional classrooms are obsolete spaces, argue that the future of education is online. According to Greene (2020), Frederick Hess, Director of Education at the American Enterprise Institute, a conservative, right-wing think tank:

> Urges that the United States' $700 billion public-education budget should be spent on "a bunch of online materials—along with a device for every child and better connectivity." Education Secretary Betsy DeVos, who has close ties with the Koch network, also sees the classroom as obsolete: "If

> our ability to educate is limited to what takes place in any given physical building, we are never going to meet the unique needs of every student."
>
> *(paragraph 5)*

More disconcerting is that the key to this newly opened door is testing:

> They're called "personalized" because an algorithm based on a student's past performance generates "learning plans" tailored to her level and interests. The student sits, encased in headphones, responding to prompts, clicking her way through preset steps to predetermined answers; she demonstrates "competencies" by passing a test, then moves on to the next task and the next test...
>
> *(paragraph 7)*

This endless barrage of assessments to determine "mastery" of content well serves edtech companies and others who maintain an instrumentalist view of education. For edtech proponents, the focus is on outputs; the inputs do not matter beyond serving as a marketing tool to entice superintendents to purchase these expensive online programs. Adding insult to injury, Glimpse K12, an edtech company, conducted a study of the $2 billion spent on technology and found that "67% of educational software product licenses go unused" (Davis, 2019, paragraph 2). Greene also cites Michael Moe, a venture capitalist, stating, "We see the education industry today as the health care industry of 30 years ago" (paragraph 4). One would imagine, from the perspective of corporations, the education industry is ripe with opportunities, waiting to be "improved" by technology. Sadly, the money flows away from serving the needs of the students, teachers and their schools into the coffers of private enterprise; as Greene aptly points out, wouldn't this money be "better spent on human resources, teachers, counselors, nurses, librarians" (paragraph 4). Thus, technology is indisputably a core element of the AIC.

Transforming schools, teachers, and students into cogs in the assessment machine created by the AIC is significant. Schools are not valued as centers of community life. They are rated based on value-added measures as determined by standardized testing. The persistence of positive perceptions of "our community schools" across the country is simultaneous with the perception of failing public education. Teachers are tasked with creating a data wall and progress monitoring formative assessment inventories. The time spent in testing has increased exponentially as exploration and creativity disappeared from classroom curricula (Hart et al., 2015). Students are represented as test scores and data (Parkison, 2009).

Good Intentions and the Road to Hell

Not all those who support education reforms do so with nefarious intent. Further, it is important to note that proponents of standardized assessments do not identify as racists. In fact, civil rights advocates and other liberal-minded leaders have lauded standardized assessments as an "objective" way to provide accountability for America's public schools. For example, in the middle of the "Great Society" initiative, Attorney General Robert Kennedy wondered about the possibilities of standardized assessments as a tool for civil rights before the U.S. Senate in 1965:

> I think it is very difficult for a person who lives in a community to know whether, in fact, his educational system is what it should be, whether if you compare his community to a neighboring community they are doing everything they should be, whether the people that are operating the educational system in a state or local community are as good as they should be…I wonder if we couldn't have some system of reporting…through some testing system that would be established (by) which the people at the local community would know periodically…what progress had been made.
>
> *(Schlesinger, 2012, p. 315)*

This rationale laid a foundation for using standardized assessment as a vehicle for social justice in schools. Paved with good intentions and enframed through the lens of standardization, assessment, and accountability, Kennedy's thinking presumes standardized tests are a valid, useful, and objective way to ensure students are learning what they should be learning.

Even in our current society, and as we already mentioned that Kendi was pointing out, those advocating for civil rights often support standardized testing. For example, one might wonder, given the documented evidence (as this book demonstrates) of the negative impacts of standardized testing, why 12 civil rights groups, in 2015, advocated for the maintenance of standardized testing requirements (Leadership Conference on Civil & Human Rights, 2015). In their 2015 press release, The Leadership Conference on Civil & Human Rights defended their opposition to anti-testing efforts because:

> Data obtained through some standardized tests are particularly important to the civil rights community because they are the only available, consistent, and objective source of data about disparities in educational outcomes, even while vigilance is always required to ensure tests are not misused. These data are used to advocate for greater resource equity in schools and more fair treatment for students of color, low-income students, students with disabilities, and English learners.
>
> *(paragraph 1)*

Yet, despite civil rights groups and others' arguments in favor of maintaining the intensity of the high-stakes testing regime, little evidence exists to support proponents' claims that these tests have mitigated disparities in educational outcomes (evidence suggests the opposite is true; Lauen & Gaddis, 2012). As for the claims that testing data is "objective" or that they reflect disparities that matter, these claims are unfounded as well. However, of all the contentions stated to support standardized testing, the one that suggests that vigilance has been given to ensure that testing data is not "misused" is a complete and utter lie (Koretz, 2017; Au, 2016). The evidence provides a different narrative, one that tells a story of not only the vicious and cruel effects of testing on our society as a whole but also and especially as it pertains to the students these civil rights groups state they want to protect. The problem is, despite good intentions, standardized tests are fundamentally racist, classist, and privileging constructs.

As noted earlier, Kendi (2016) underscores the relationship between standardized testing and civil rights leaders' call for testing as a means of accountability. But he also demonstrates another relationship, that between the desire to close the achievement gap and "opening the door to racist ideas" (paragraph 14). Kendi (2016) inquires:

> But what if, all along, our well-meaning efforts at closing the achievement gap has been opening the door to racist ideas? What if different environments actually cause different kinds of achievement rather than different levels of achievement? What if the intellect of a poor, low testing Black child in a poor Black school is different—and not inferior—to the intellect of a rich, high-testing White child in a rich White school? What if the way we measure intelligence shows not only our racism but our elitism?
>
> *(paragraph 14)*

For Kendi, it is a matter of what constitutes the definition of achievement and intellect. Taking this a step further, we may inquire as to why civil rights leaders, who are co-opted into thinking that standardized testing truly represents superior knowledge, intellect, and capacity, believe this rather than believe that it is a system that supports racial hierarchies and racism.

Like any construct that we utilize, the origins of that construct have the potential to be freight in the biases and blind spots from which they grew. In other words, some civil rights leaders may be utilizing a neoliberal lens to interpret the value of standardized testing rather than, let's say, an ecological or humanistic one. Even if we account for the bias of standardized testing, some implicit and some explicit, is this how we, as a society, want to measure student learning and success? Even if we do attempt to reform standardized tests to account for biases, might not "standardized tests" (given their standardization against the mean, and the mean being White) remain inherently racist at their core? Another question one might pose is: Shouldn't we design assessments to measure actual student learning and various intellectual strengths that are equally valued and occurring in different contexts? As Singer posits (2019, April 6), "After all, what is a standardized test but an assessment that refers to a specific standard? And that standard is white, upper class students" (paragraph 37). As the AIC anchors all educational decisions, that anchor is weighed by racist notions of what it means to be a standard human.

Assessment Meets Neoliberal Washington Consensus: The Path to Omnishambles

The assumption that standardized tests are impartial allows the testing industry to capitalize on well-intended education policy. Thus, testing and test preparation have become the manufactured gold standard for what counts for knowledge and learning across educational institutions throughout the United States. The AIC determines what counts for knowing through standardized tests; consequently, the U.S. education system is left in omnishambles. The term "omnishambles," as defined by the Cambridge Dictionary (n.d.), means "a situation that is bad in many different ways, because things have been organized badly and serious mistakes have been made" (paragraph 1). These omnishambles have been enabled and perpetuated by what Noam Chomsky (1999) calls "neoliberal Washington consensus":

> An array of market-oriented principles designed by the government of the United States and international financial institutions that it largely dominates, and implemented by them in various ways- for more vulnerable societies, often as stringent structural adjustment programs. The basic rules, in brief are: liberalize trade, finance, let markets set the price ("get prices right"), end inflation (microeconomic stability), privatize. The government should "get out of the way"—hence the population too, insofar as the government is democratic, though the conclusion remains implicit. The decisions of those who impose "consensus" naturally have a major impact on the global order. (pp. 19–20)

Under this ideology, public schools and other democratic institutions are susceptible to impositions of "consensus" that public institutions are failing and can only be fixed through free-market principles. Though the term "neoliberalism" dates back to the late 19th century, neoliberal Washington consensus began to garner wide bipartisan support 40 years ago.

Neoliberal ideas drastically spread after the 1980 U.S. Presidential election; Ronald Reagan led the charge to reduce tax rates and domestic programs from the "Great Society" initiative of the 1960s, all the while raising defense spending to historical levels. Reagan, a former Hollywood actor and California Governor, used easy-to-understand rhetoric. For example, to teach the American public that the private can and should replace the public, Reagan simply stated, "the nine most terrifying words in the English language are, I'm from the government and

I'm here to help'" (Reagan, 1990). Reagan based this argument on the assumption that the federal government is inefficient, and the free market can offer a better deal to taxpayers. This premise, sometimes referred to as Reaganomics, asserts that people can use the money they would have paid in taxes to invest in the free market. Reagan argued the tax cuts should mostly go to corporations because they can reinvest those savings in both creating jobs and spending.

Consequently, under Reagan, globalization further expanded. Watergate was yesterday's news, the economy was experiencing a recession, and the Cold War still dominated foreign policy. Reagan, who some refer to as "The Great Communicator," used his sense of humor and charm to significantly direct U.S. policy toward an era that harkens back to unfettered capitalism, all the while borrowing historically high amounts of credit to fund tax cuts and defense spending. Though the merits of this approach deserve criticism and debate, it is beyond the scope of this chapter. Relevant to this argument, however, is that Reagan's style of simple communication helped orient a broad range of the American public, including longtime Democrats, toward a neoliberal ideology—even if it went against their own political and economic interests.

In his campaign rhetoric, Reagan promised to abolish the U.S. Department of Education, which his predecessor and election opponent, Jimmy Carter, had recently created. Reagan charged the newly appointed U.S. Secretary of Education, T.H. Bell, to form an 18-person committee, the National Commission on Excellence in Education, to investigate the quality of teaching and learning in the United States. Their findings were presented in a well-known and often cited report known as *A Nation at Risk* (National Commission on Excellence in Education, 1983). The report highlighted drops in overall SAT scores and deficiencies in reading, writing, and math to argue that a rising tide of mediocrity has left American public education in a downward trajectory, and, without action, these trends would undermine economic and military interests. Although other studies, like "Perspectives on Education in America" (also known as the "Sandia Report"; Huelskamp, 1993), drew stark contrasts from the findings and analysis in *A Nation at Risk*, hyperbolic rhetoric of failing schools captured the American psyche (Berliner & Biddle, 1996). Corporate media outlets deemed public education as a failure, and politicians promised reform (Schwartz, Robinson, Kirst, & Kirp, 2000).

By 1989, and as a result of subsequent reforms, public discourse of education began to focus on the productivity and effectiveness of public education. Productivity would soon function as a framework by which citizens came to understand the effectiveness of schooling (e.g., outcomes-based education). In addition, President George H. W. Bush promised to promote education reform and offered a vision, *America 2000*, to improve school productivity, which proposed minimum competency tests in fourth, eighth, and twelfth grade (Superfine, 2005). Although Congress did not pass *America 2000*, it laid the foundation for President Bill Clinton to create *Goals 2000*. *Goals 2000: Educate America Act* provided the requisite legislation to promote education reformers' agenda of imbuing state accountability systems across the United States. The argument states, as Loveless (2005) posits, that if we provide rigorous content standards to teachers for their students, and we hold students accountable for learning those standards, then education will improve. By the turn of the century, 49 out of the 50 states had standardized assessments in place (Hoffman, Assaf, & Paris, 2001), which eventually provided the *No Child Left Behind Act* of 2001 (U.S. Department of Education, 2002) the necessary infrastructure to hold individual schools accountable for meeting state content standards—a political promise from George W. Bush's presidential campaign. This ideology would continue into the Obama Administration, including initiatives like *Race to the Top* (Tenam-Zemach & Flynn, 2011) and the adoption of Common Core Standards by, at one point, 42 states as well as the District of Columbia.

The Anti-Democratic Rhetoric of the AIC

The AIC also uses a web of alternative narratives to justify its approach to circumventing democratic and constitutional process and have been spreading these narratives using ideologically loyal and controlled public and private media institutions. Conspiracy theories, defamation campaigns, and hate speech against voices of dissent have assumed central positions in this web. To further expand its control, the AIC has come to increase its rhetoric on notions of pseudo-wellness and differential instruction that tighten its grip on many aspects of societal life—under the pretense that they are ruling on behalf of ordinary citizens and attending to their needs.

In the public space, the AIC attempts to silence voices of dissent and pro-democracy groups. The AIC has internalized the linkage between participation and consciousness that structure the application of power and powerlessness, which facilitates its continued hegemony (Benhabib, 2002, 2004). The AIC regime has sought to discredit these voices and groups to break any conceptual link among democracy, human rights, and the interests of ordinary people. Moreover, the same techniques are used to discredit activists critical of wide-scale human rights abuses and teachers, as well as other labor groups, demanding legitimate wage increases and changes in working conditions for themselves, their students, and their constituents. One unique example of the threat of suppression of voices beyond the AIC, but representative of the same dogma and constituency, is currently being witnessed in the streets of America. Protestors, both peaceful and violent, are demanding that injustices against Black and Brown bodies be acknowledged and remedied. Yet, former President Trump responded to these pleas for justice with comments such as "You Loot, We Shoot" (Frum, 2020) and threats of deploying the military if governors do not gain control of the protestors. While we acknowledge that violence may not be an effective response to the killing of innocent people of color and police brutality, we "understand why those individuals have taken to the streets: 'A riot,' King said, 'is the language of the unheard'" (Rothman, 2015). Eve Ewing (2018), in her poign-antly narrated text, *Ghosts in the Schoolyard: Racism and School Closings in Chicago's Southside,* discusses the silencing of community voices in the face of school closings and the impact it had on the African-American community. In her narrative, Ewing offers a perspective of the effects of hegemony on those who are powerless to defeat the powerful no matter how much they scream, shout and fight to protect their schools. She describes their need to be heard and for what they are fighting: "Community members are fighting for an acknowledgment of past harms, an honest reckoning of present injustice, and an acceptance of their reality—a reality in which a school's value is about much more than numbers" (p. 124). Nevertheless, Rahm Emanuel and the Chicago Public School Board closed down many of the schools that activists fought to save, using testing data to justify school closures.

Also insidious, as ideologically loyal and controlled media outlets tell it, local and international reports documenting human rights abuses and narrating the personal tragedies of activists are outright lies. For these outlets, statements issued by watchdog organizations, internal bureaucracies, and opposition leaders detailing the regime's repressive policies or corrupt actions are all manifestations of grand con-spiracies against not only the AIC but the country. Reliance on and use of the AIC often allows the administration to dismiss universal standards of democracy and the rule of law as practices pushed by enemies that are not binding to the adminis-tration. Various rights abuses are all committed under the banner of protecting the nation and defending the interests of ordinary, legal Americans (Benhabib, 2011). The AIC, like all effective advertising, distracts attention from policy impact and value implications. The spectacle is meant to facilitate loyalty and compliance. As citizens who are active participants in the democratic dialogue of this nation, it is our responsibility to consider what brand we are giving our loyalty.

References

Au, W. (2016). Meritocracy 2.0: High-stakes, standardized testing as a racial project of neoliberal multiculturalism. *Educational Policy*, *30*(1), 39–62.

Au, W. W. (2009). High-stakes testing and discursive control: The triple bind for non-standard student identities. *Multicultural Perspectives*, *11*(2), 65–71.

Benhabib, S. (2000). *The reluctant modernism of Hannah Arendt.* Lanham, MD: Rowman & Littlefield Publishers, Inc.

Benhabib, S. (2002). *The claims of culture: Equality and diversity in the global era.* Princeton, NJ: Princeton University Press.

Benhabib, S. (2004). *The rights of others: Aliens, residents, and citizens.* Cambridge, UK: Cambridge University Press.

Benhabib, S. (2011). *Dignity in adversity: Human rights in turbulent times.* Cambridge, MA: Polity Press.

Berliner, D. C., & Biddle, B. J. (1996). The manufactured crisis: Myths, fraud, and the attack on America's public schools, *Nassp Bulletin*, *80*(576), 119–121.

Bullitt County History. (n.d.). *1912 school exam.* Retrieved from https://www. bullittcountyhistory.com/bchistory/schoolexam1912.html.

Cambridge Dictionary. (n.d.). *Omnishambles: Definition in the Cambridge English Dictionary.* Retrieved from https://dictionary.cambridge.org/us/dictionary/english/omnishambles.

Cascio, E. U., & Washington, E. (2013). Valuing the vote: The redistribution of voting rights and state funds following the Voting Rights Act of 1965. *The Quarterly Journal of Economics, 129*(1), 379–433.

Chomsky, C. (1995, January–May). Rollback. *Z Magazine.* Retrieved from https:// chomsky.info/199505__/#TXT2.23.

Chomsky, N. (1999). *Profit over people: Neoliberalism and global order.* New York, NY: Seven Stories Press.

Connor, K., & Vargyas, E. J. (1992). The legal implications of gender bias in standardized testing. *Berkeley Women's LJ, 7,* 13–89.

Davis, M. R. (2019, May 14). *K-12 districts wasting millions by not using purchased software, new analysis finds. EdWeek Market Brief.* Retrieved from https://marketbrief.edweek. org/marketplace-k-12/unused-educational-software-major-source-wasted-k-12-spending-new-analysis-finds/.

Derrida, J. (1989). *Of spirit: Heidegger & the question* (G. Bennington & R. Bowlby, Trans.). Chicago, IL: The University of Chicago Press.

Dowbiggin, I. R. (1997). *Keeping America sane: Psychiatry and eugenics in the United States and Canada* (pp. 1880–1940). Ithaca, NY: Cornell University Press.

Ewing, E. L. (2018). *Ghosts in the schoolyard: Racism and school closings on Chicago's south side.* Chicago, IL: University of Chicago Press.

Farin, I. & Malpas, J. (Eds.). (2018). *Reading Heidegger's black notebooks: 1931–1941.* Cambridge, MA: MIT Press.

Filer, J. E., Kenny, L. W., & Morton, R. B. (1991). Voting laws, educational policies, and minority turnout, *The Journal of Law and Economics, 34*(2, Part 1), 371–393.

Frum, D. (2020, May 29). *Trump is the Looter: The president is exposing problems in America that most did not want to see. The Atlantic.* Retrieved from https://www.theatlantic.com/ ideas/archive/2020/05/trump-exposes-america-we-didnt-want-see/612331/.

Galton, F. (1904). Eugenics: Its definition, scope, and aims. *American Journal of Sociology, 10*(1), 1–25.

Gaventa, J. (1980). *Power and powerlessness: Quiescence and rebellion in an Appalachian valley.* Urbana, IL: University of Illinois Press.

Giordano, G. (2005). *How testing came to dominate American schools: The history of educational assessment.* New York, NY: Peter Lang.

Gould, S. J. (1994, November 28). Curveball. *The New Yorker.* Retrieved from https:// www.dartmouth.edu/~chance/course/topics/curveball.html.

Graves, J. L. (2001). *The emperor's new clothes.* New Brunswick:Rutgers University Press.

Greene, G. (2020, August 10). *Ed tech cashes in on the pandemic. The American Prospect.* Retrieved from https://prospect.org/education/ed-tech-cashes-in-on-the-pandemic/.

Hart, R., Casserly, M., Uzzell, R., Palacios, M., Corcoran, A., & Spurgeon, L. (2015). *Student testing in America's great city schools: An inventory and preliminary analysis [White paper].* Council of the Great City Schools. Retrieved from https://www.cgcs.org/cms/ lib/DC00001581/Centricity/Domain/87/Testing%20Report.pdf.

Heckman, James J. (1995). Lessons from the Bell Curve. *Journal of Political Economy, 103*(5), 1091–1120. 10.1086/262014

Heidegger, M. (1977). *The question concerning technology, and other essays* (W. Levitt, Trans.). New York, NY: Harper & Row.

Herrnstein, R. J., & Murray, C. (1994). *The bell curve: Intelligence and class structure in American life*. New York, NY: Free Press.

Hoffman, Assaf, & Paris (2001). High-stakes testing in reading: Today in Texas, tomorrow? *The Reading Teacher, 54*(3), 482–492.

Holley, C. E. (1920). *Mental tests for school use*. Chicago: University of Illinois.

Holocaust Encyclopedia. (n.d.). *Victims of the Nazi era: Nazi racial ideology*. Retrieved from https://encyclopedia.ushmm.org/content/en/article/victims-of-the-nazi-era-nazi-racial-ideology.

Huelskamp, R. M. (1993). Perspectives on education in America. *The Phi Delta Kappan, 74*(9), 718–721.

Kendi, I. X. (2016, October 20). *Why the academic achievement gap is a racist idea. Black Perspectives*. Retrieved from https://www.aaihs.org/why-the-academic-achievement-gap-is-a-racist-idea/.

Kendi, I. X. (2019). *How to be an antiracist*. New York, NY: Random House.

Knoester, M., & Au, W. (2017). Standardized testing and school segregation: Like tinder for fire? *Race Ethnicity and Education, 20*(1), 1–14.

Koretz, D. (2017). *The testing charade: Pretending to make schools better*. Chicago, IL: University of Chicago Press.

Kristeva, J. (2001). *Hannah Arendt: Life is a narrative* (F. Collins, Trans.). Toronto, Canada: University of Toronto Press.

Lauen, D., & Gaddis, S. (2012). Shining a light or fumbling in the dark? The effects of NCLB's subgroup-specific accountability on student achievement. *Educational Evaluation and Policy Analysis, 34*(2), 185–208.

Leadership Conference on Civil & Human Rights. (2015). *Civil rights groups: "We oppose anti-testing efforts."* Retrieved from https://civilrights.org/2015/05/05/civil-rights-groups-we-oppose-anti-testing-efforts/.

Lombardo, P. A. (Ed.). (2011). *A century of eugenics in America: from the Indiana experiment to the human genome era*. Bloomington: Indiana University Press.

Loveless, T. (2005). Test-based accountability: The promise and the perils. *Brookings Papers on Education Policy, 8*, 7–45.

Mitchell, A. J. & Trawny, P. (Eds.). (2017). *Heidegger's black notebooks: Responses to Anti-Semitism*. New York, NY: Columbia University Press.

Mueller, C. (1972). *The politics of communication: A study of the political sociology of language, socialization and legitimation*. Oxford, UK: Oxford University Press.

National Commission on Excellence in Education. (1983). *A nation at risk: The imperative for educational reform*. Retrieved from https://edreform.com/wp-content/uploads/2013/02/A_Nation_At_Risk_1983.pdf.

Parkison, P. (2009). Political economy of NCLB: Standards, testing and test scores. *The Educational Forum, 73*(1), 44–57.

Peterson, P. E. (2010). *Saving schools: From Horace Mann to virtual learning*. Cambridge, MA: Harvard University Press.

Reagan, R. (1990). *Ronald Reagan: An American life*. New York, NY: Simon & Schuster.

Reese, W. J. (2013). *Testing wars in the public schools: A forgotten history*. Cambridge, MA: Harvard University Press.

Roberts, H. E., & Skinner, J. (1996). Gender and racial equity of the Air Force Officer Qualifying Test in officer training school selection decis. *Military Psychology, 8*(2), 95–113.

Rodgers III, W. M., & Spriggs, W. E. (1996). What does the AFQT really measure: Race, wages, schooling and the AFQT score. *The Review of Black Political Economy, 24*(4), 13–46.

Roid, G. H., & Pomplun, M. (2012). *The Stanford-Binet Intelligence Scales.* New York, NY: The Guilford Press.

Rothman, L. (2015, April 28). What Martin Luther King Jr. really thought about riots. *Time.* Retrieved from https://time.com/3838515/baltimore-riots-language-unheard-quote/.

Rothman, R. (2001). One hundred fifty years of testing. In L. Iura (Ed.), *The Jossey-Bass reader on school reform* (pp. 419–433). San Francisco, CA: Wiley Company.

Schlesinger, A. M. (2012). *Robert Kennedy and his times.* Boston, MA: Houghton Mifflin Harcourt.

Schwartz, R. B., Robinson, M. A., Kirst, M. W., & Kirp, D. L. (2000). Goals 2000 and the standards movement. *Brookings papers on education policy, 3*, 173–214.

Shanklin, E. (1994). *Anthropology and race.* Belmont, CA: Wadsworth.

Shirer, W. L. (1960). *The rise and fall of the Third Reich: A history of Nazi Germany.* New York, NY: Simon and Schuster.

Singer, S. (2019, April 06). *Standardized testing is a tool of white supremacy. Common Dreams.* Retrieved from https://www.commondreams.org/views/2019/04/06/standardized-testing-tool-white-supremacy.

Stoskopf, A. (2002). Echoes of a forgotten past: Eugenics, testing, and education reform. *The Educational Forum, 66*(2), 126–133.

Stovall, D. O. (2016). *Born out of struggle: Critical race theory, school creation, and the politics of interruption.* Albany, NY: Suny Press.

Superfine, B. M. (2005). The politics of accountability: The rise and fall of Goals 2000. *American Journal of Education, 112*(1), 10–43.

Tenam-Zemach, M., & Flynn, J. (2011). America's race to the top, our fall from grace. *Curriculum & Teaching Dialogue, 13*(1/2), 113–124.

U.S. Department of Education. (2002). *No child left behind, accountability and AYP.* Retrieved from https://www2.ed.gov/admins/lead/account/nclbreference/reference.pdf.

U.S. Department of Education. (2009). *Race to the top executive summary.* Retrieved from https://www2.ed.gov/programs/racetothetop/executive-summary.pdf.

Valentine, L. D. Jr. (1977). *Prediction of Air Force technical training success from ASVAB and educational background.* Air Force Human Resources Lab. Retrieved from https://apps.dtic.mil/dtic/tr/fulltext/u2/a041735.pdf.

Winfield, A. G. (2007). *Eugenics and education in America: Institutionalized racism and the implications of history, ideology, and memory* (Vol. 18). New York, NY: Peter Lang.

3

STRANGE BEDFELLOWS

How Test-Driven Accountability Became Common Sense

To understand how the Assessment Industrial Complex (AIC) became a complex, we first must delineate the reasons both sides of the political aisle came to see testing as dovetailing with their pet concerns. The need to hold institutions accountable, and the role of testing in that process, emerged in force toward the end of the 1970s, amid a few converging historical trends. First, the domestic economic boom that followed the close of World War II had begun to slow (Westbury, 1984), a process that involved a series of energy crises, gas shortages, a slow manufacturing decline, and the stirrings of globalization. The national sense of precarity, of an urgent need to prepare ourselves for a shift in the alignment of global economics, underwrote the tone and tenor of the *Nation at Risk* report. The first sentence infamously compared the "rising tide of mediocrity" in our schools with a foreign adversary's "act of war" upon us (The National Commission on Excellence in Education, 1983, p. 1). The experimental pedagogies and organizational strategies of the 1960s and 1970s—open classrooms, enhanced local control, multicultural curricula—suddenly seemed intolerably inattentive to the needs of a competitive, soon to be globalized future, from the perspectives of individual students and the nation alike (Goldstein, 2015; Ravitch, 2010).

This sense of precarity, and the education system's responsibility for addressing it, has extended into today's educational milieu. For instance, American journalist and commentator, Nicholas Kristof (2012), advocated that states include the data from their annual high-stakes tests in *teacher* evaluations, insisting that "America's economy and national well-being" depended on it (paragraph 6). When Linda Darling-Hammond (2015) suggests that the persistent racial achievement gap is harmful, she speaks of it as threatening America's global economic competitiveness. This kind of rhetoric heightens and maintains the urgency of *knowing*, in a wide and general sense, what kind of education the future will require and whether our schools are performing adequately toward that end. This rhetoric is also the primary means through which the public participates in education, and thus a primary factor in the formation of the public consciousness around education. Education is framed as an individual economic lever, not at a common interest or good.

Second, after the emergence of the "Great Society" program in the 1960s, the Right recognized the public's hesitation to support expanding social welfare policies. "Conservatives regularly criticized the Great Society programs as ill-conceived, immoral, and wasteful" (O'Connor, 2003, p. 49). Additionally, the political right implemented two rhetorical approaches to articulating their opposition to the New Deal's welfare state, which implicated a significant portion of publicly administered arms of government, including schools (Skowronek, 1982, p. 288). The first was to suggest that incompetence and mismanagement were rife throughout systems of public administration. Ronald Reagan's successful use of the figure of the "welfare queen" to signify the sorts of fraud and waste that supposedly beset the system as a whole is sufficient to show the effectiveness of the rhetorical claim that unaccountable bureaucrats needed some kind of oversight. At the same time, the political Right was learning to leverage the social justice language emerging from the Civil Rights movement for their ends. As the Great Society's social programs were developed and implemented, the combination of broad political consensus and weak partisanship that had characterized American politics since the New Deal began to unravel.

The electoral success of the Republican party in the 1980s can be seen mainly as the consequence of this strategic rhetorical shift. As several scholars previously identified, the "Reagan Revolution" shifted social policy debates to the benefit of the political Right, a shift that included "increasingly negative framing of discussions about welfare recipients" (Hacker, 2002; O'Connor, 2003, p. 188; Skocpol, 1996). In fact, much of President Reagan's political agenda and subsequent success can be understood as a result of these changes. As Weaver (2000) describes, conservative critics suggested that social policies, including public education policies, "caused more problems for poor families than it solved, encouraging out-of-wedlock births, discouraging marriage and work, and helping to create a socially and economically isolated underclass that transmitted poverty from generation to generation" (p. 104). Hence, "conservative diagnoses and prescriptions...were part of a broader conservative renaissance that began in the 1970s and gained momentum with the election of Ronald Reagan" in 1980 (Weaver, 2000, p. 104).

This shift in public consciousness, from widespread consensus to uncertainty, opened a door of political opportunity for the political right to pursue a conservative narrative in which social issues were increasingly viewed as external to government responsibility. The publication of Michael Harrington's book, *The Other America*, stimulated a national debate about poverty in post-war America, and public support for liberal economic policies waned (O'Connor, 2003). The failures of the Great Society reforms were thus used as justifications for reducing the federal government's involvement in the social arena. As O'Connor (2003) notes, the political right in the 1970s became "very effective at turning criticisms of the welfare state into right-wing arguments about failures of the welfare state" (p. 56). The Right could therefore use the same kind of rhetoric to pursue their broader agenda that the Left had used in the 1960s to protect the rights of women and African-Americans.

The political dominance of the Republican Party in presidential elections throughout this period indicated a need for Democrats to cater more to conservative values, particularly in the realm of social policy. Thus, to separate himself from the legacy of Great Society programs, Bill Clinton incorporated the "New Democrat" label during his victorious 1992 presidential campaign (O'Connor, 2003, p. 190). This novel political identity describes an ideologically centrist political platform that could more effectively compete with highly influential conservative narratives. As Martin Walker (1996) suggests, "A New Democrat was tough on crime, tough on welfare, resolute about the death penalty, and insisted on personal responsibility rather than state handouts" (p. 333). To complement Clinton's political centrism, the Democratic Leadership Council (DLC), of which Clinton was both a founder and former chairman, created the Progressive Policy Institute (PPI) to "examine national problems that were under debate in Congress" (Lyman, 2000, p. 48) and develop politically moderate solutions for them.

However, after the Republican Revolution in 1994 provided Republicans with unified congressional control, Clinton and the DLC largely submitted to the desires of the political right and incorporated conservative social policy preferences within the broader Democratic platform, particularly in the realm of education. To do so, Clinton and his allied organizations developed an effective partnership for establishing national social policies that "split the difference" between the two parties, ultimately seeking to "please the greatest number of people by offering ideas that offended the fewest" (Lyman, 2000, p. 47). This was particularly true in the realm of education, where New Democrats advocated policies that both disadvantaged minority students and further centralized systems of public education at the federal level. As Lyman (2000) asserts, "in addition to supporting charter schools, the DLC has called for voluntary national academic standards, more teacher accountability, and an end to social promotion" (p. 49). Hence, Clinton's presidency represents a significant turning point in terms of the striking similarities between the two parties on educational policy development.

One effective example of this rhetorical manipulation is the Right's use of social-justice language across domains of public administration: their argument of "taxpayer rights." Whether in the criminal justice system (Murakawa, 2014; Schoenfeld, 2018) or in welfare administration (Tani, 2016), rights language constructed tax-paying citizens as vulnerable to the specific harm of mismanaged resources at the hands of government bureaucrats, failing to deliver on taxpayers' reasonable expectation of a certain return on their investment in the public. The problem, rhetorically speaking, was one of inadequate oversight and responsiveness. As the American education system hobbled along, no one knew exactly how well it was doing, but the crisis rhetoric (Berliner & Biddle, 1996) made Americans sit up and wonder. Meanwhile, no one was protecting the taxpayer, the one who contributed all the resources, the one who had a right to expect certain results. The parallel to the shift from a stakeholder perspective toward a shareholder perspective is central to the entrenchment of neoliberalism. With the payment of taxes, we all become shareholders in the corporation that is our government—local, state, and federal. Moreover, the taxpayer had a right to demand that the education system, as well as other publicly-administered systems, provide transparent progress reports to avoid the possibilities of systematic waste or idiosyncratic whim determining outcomes for students.

Extending the model of shareholder accountability into the realm of education is significant in the shifting view of education as in the public sphere. Shareholder theory is primarily based on the idea that the primary purpose of a business is generating profits and increasing shareholder wealth. Shareholder theory relies heavily on the fiduciary duty between the company's directors and the company's shareholders. The United States' version of the modern shareholder approach picked up steam in 1970 with Milton Friedman's article, The Social Responsibility of Business is to Increase its Profits (1970). Friedman laid out that "there is one and only one social responsibility of business—to use its resources and engage in activities designed to increase its profits so long as it stays within the rules of the game…" (paragraph 34). This view takes the approach that solving social problems is the responsibility of the state. Followers of this theory believe that if businesses use wealth for social and moral developments, it will negatively impact society in the future. The extension of shareholder accountability into public education marks a vital shift—neoliberalism privatizes the public sphere, making everything a private good.

Unlike the shareholder approach, the stakeholder theory has its roots in the late 1970s and early 1980s when researchers with backgrounds in philosophy, psychology, sociology, and management began to challenge some of the basic assumptions of classic economics and shareholder theory. The stakeholder approach is founded on the idea that when taking the interests of all the stakeholders into account, the institution could achieve greater performance than by merely focusing on shareholder interests. Stakeholders are individuals and constituencies that contribute, either voluntarily or involuntarily, to an institution's wealth-creating capacity and activities; and, they are, therefore, its potential beneficiaries and/or risk bearers. It is grounded in the concept that if an institution creates value for stakeholders, it creates value for shareholders. Within education, this would mean that if a school is serving the needs of the students, families, and community, it would be best serving the needs of the political elite. The stakeholder approach, unlike shareholder theory, emphasizes an ethical responsibility to the community and an understanding of an institution's impact on the community. Adopting the share-holder perspective, the AIC has informed educational ethics. As stated above, the ethical emerges within the relational condition of care (or what we care about) that accompanies our experiences in the world. This care is contextual, and it emerges as a consequence of the conceptual frame from which we start—seeing students, teachers, and community members as stakeholders can be dramatically different than focusing concern on business leaders and policymakers as shareholders. Having a clear understanding of our conceptual framing within either a shareholder or a stakeholder perspective informs how we understand the measures used and the audience to which we are accountable.

The idea that accountability grounded in shareholder ethics that was being demanded of other public systems was also necessary to help public schools meet their responsibilities and was advocated for early on within the education pro-fession itself. In 1978, Kentucky Principal Irvin K. Rice was already suggesting that the experimentalism associated with "modular scheduling and open class-rooms" (Rice, 1978, p. 10) was distracting the educational infrastructure from its central purpose and, therefore, inadequately addressing the needs of its "clients." For Rice, that central purpose was "adult competency," and, because "the tool of social science in a democracy seems to be statistical analysis" (p. 10), he argued that standardized testing was best-positioned to provide the grist for an ac-countability mill: "the coefficient of accountability," he said, "must be a quan-tification reflective of education's purpose" (p. 10). The need for governmental transparency and accountability was widespread across bureaucratic domains. In the educational sphere, that seemed to require focusing on a singular purpose that schools ought to serve and test students so that the state could see and demon-strate whether schools were living up to their responsibility. William Bost (1978) called for a similar degree of clarity in the purpose of public schooling, and he directly tied his exhortation to the idea of taxpayers' rights: "Taxpayers are saying they have had enough of runaway costs and not much to show for it. School boards are getting hard-nosed about both budgets and productivity" (p. 243). Bost's solution was also closely aligned with Rice's. He suggested, "that we disavow responsibility for tackling every social ill that besets the American people" and instead "become serious about specifying and clarifying our re-sponsibilities to the next generation of adults" (p. 244). "Accountability," based on testing, was designed to access a "quantification reflective of education's purpose" (p. 10). It would help to slow down the wild proliferation of untested pedagogical and organizational methods, rein in bureaucratic waste, and provide taxpayers with the knowledge and the leverage to demand changes in otherwise unresponsive schools, should schools indeed fall behind in their responsibilities.

The political left, meanwhile, was just as interested as the political right in ensuring that the public education system was appropriately responsive to its task; though, the left's fears of unresponsiveness were rooted in a different place. The lesson, for the left, of the transition from a *Plessy v. Ferguson* to *Brown v. Board of*

Education, was that "equality" could have significantly different political meanings (Moses, 2016). The decade after the *Brown* decision, the era of "massive resistance" (Suitts, 2019), only enforced the left's traditional comfort with using federal power to protect the equal rights of African-Americans, particularly in the face of Southern recalcitrance. The specter of differential treatment based on race—again, in both criminal justice and in education—helped to align the political left with a project of procedural standardization intended to counter racial prejudice (Murakawa, 2014).

The 1954 *Brown* decision had mainly depended on the evidence of harm from the Clarks' "doll studies," in which Black children were shown to associate positive characteristics with white dolls and negative characteristics with black ones. The associations implied that segregation was producing harm to Black children's self-concepts. If the theory was that desegregating schools could prevent this particular harm, that was not the same as ensuring that schools were fulfilling their positive duties concerning all students equally. In fact, bell hooks 1994 and Lisa Delpit (1995) both suggest that desegregation created new kinds of issues for Black children (and Black teachers). It was a further question of whether schools were adequately meeting the specific educational needs of all students, and the political left was comfortable with the use of state (and federal) oversight to ensure that schools and districts were not differentially educating their students based on race. The criterion, the evidence, for this sort of question obviously could not take the same form like the one in the doll studies. For an entity as distant from a particular context as a state or federal government to claim to *see* whether schools were adequately discharging their responsibilities, something else would be necessary, something like a "quantification…of education's purpose," in Principal Rice's words.

When George W. Bush advocated for the *No Child Left Behind Act* (NCLB) in 2001, the law that federally required that each state tests students in grades 3–8 and once again in high school, he summoned the language of inequality to reinforce its bipartisan nature. Testing, he implied, in an echo of Delpit's 1995 worries, would prevent the "soft bigotry of low expectations" (Bush, 2000, n. p.) from interfering with the learning of Black students. The state assessments, and the federal requirement to disaggregate scores by race, gender, first language, disability status, and SES, framed potential *gaps*. These gaps were determined solely on testing data, as achievement levers by which social justice advocates could make demands on schools and the public entities that ran them.

The appearance of advocating for social justice was the AICs main appeal to the left. By producing evidence that specifically looked for inequalities along the lines of longstanding injustice, tests provided a means by which activists could hold prejudiced school officials to account for living up to the promises of equality in public education. The AICs appeal to the political right was only different in the party to which it addressed itself. Tests would make school performance publicly transparent, and taxpayer organizations could use those results to ensure that schools were delivering the right bang for the taxpayers' buck. In both cases, achievement data derived from standardized tests fed public interest in the interest of American educational quality—and equality. The same information, the same data, could be wielded by the right to check the efficiency of an otherwise insufficient accountable public bureaucracy, and by the left, to check the justice of an otherwise insufficiently accountable local school officials.

Rhetoric to Manufacture Endless Crises

Through the use of the rhetoric of the AIC and its myths and symbols of crisis in the realm of education, the powerful have been able to ensure that certain beliefs and actions emerge in one context while contradictory grievances are repressed in others. Ultimately, the use of testing data to prop up a new system of account-ability coalesced the political left and right around a common goal: to use stan-dardized testing to pressure systems of education to respond to the manufactured crisis of failure. Failure in this context was limited to how students performed on their state exams. To be clear, while there certainly are a plethora of inequalities across and within educational systems (e.g., inequitable school funding; lack of access to mental health counselors; high teacher turnover, class size variability, etc.), these inequalities are systemic and much more profound than any given assessment or test can measure or account for.

Thus, both the political right and left came together around the idea of "closing the achievement gap." Sen. Ted Kennedy (D) and several other Congressional Representatives, as well as a diverse group of young children, looked on as President George W. Bush (R) signed the NCLB into law. It was a photo opportunity for the ages, a perceived victory in bipartisan, accountability in the "name of" social justice. Simultaneously, this new piece of federal legislation gave the U.S. Department of Education leverage to force states into mandating standardized testing. As Weir et al. (1988) have suggested, the American federal state provides enhanced leverage to those political interests able to associate across many local political districts. Education has long been perceived as a collective interest in which all citizens hold a substantive stake (Weir et al., 1988). By combining this collective interest with the capacity to associate varying political constituencies across local districts within states, NCLB, similar to other educa-tion policies that followed it, provided both sides of the political aisle with the opportunity to incorporate AIC initiatives in their platforms to both their benefit. The notion of "accountability," and the use of standardized tests to conduct it, therefore, appealed to both sides of the political spectrum simultaneously.

The bipartisan compromise on accountability policy mostly held through the administration of Barack Obama, although cracks were plainly visible by Obama's second term. By 2009, certain flaws in NCLBs technical requirements were ap-parent. The law had required states to create a plan to help all of their students reach proficiency in math and reading by 2014 (U.S. Department of Education, 2002).

That meant that states, schools, and teachers were highly, and strictly, incentivized to attend to students at or near the proficiency cut score in any given year, the students whose proficiency status was in doubt. Schools could count on students who had tested well above the proficiency line the year before to do so again, regardless of the quality of the school's education. And school administrators and teachers likewise knew that students who had tested far, far below the proficiency cut score had little hope of reaching that bar in the space of a single year, no matter the quality of the school's education. The resulting focus on the "bubble kids" (Booher-Jennings, 2005), to the exclusion of the high- and low-performing students, unintentionally created a new axis of inequality that needed to be addressed. Similarly, the law required that *schools*, as whole buildings, be held accountable for the performance of their students, even though emerging research showed tremendous variability in teachers' individual impact on student learning (Chetty, Friedman, & Rockoff, 2011, 2014; Kane et al., 2008; McCaffrey et al., 2009). In both cases, NCLB seemed to be paying inadequate attention to individual teachers and students.

The Obama administration used stimulus money appropriated in the wake of the 2008 financial crisis to incentivize state-level tweaks to the way states implemented test-based accountability. Although NCLB was still technically in force, the Obama administration's *Race to the Top* Program promised waivers from NCLBs punitive sanctions, as well as a significant amount of money, to states willing and able to change the laws on their books following the administration's wishes. These changes included adopting a set of de-facto national standards (Tampio, 2018); changing the laws around teacher evaluation and tenure so that "teacher quality" was tied to student achievement; giving local administrators a freer hand to hire and fire on that basis, and altering the determination of whether a school was making adequate yearly progress from a status measure (which focused on bubble kids) to a growth measure (in which all students' expected growth would matter).

These changes, too, generally appealed to both sides of the political spectrum. Taking accountability down to the level of the individual teacher, empowering administrators to make sweeping personnel changes and evading union-driven collective bargaining agreements, and so on, spoke to the political right's concern with governmental agility and efficiency when held to specific standards. Ensuring that all students' achievement data counted for accountability purposes assured the political left that teachers' attention would be distributed equitably inside the classroom. But there was unrest, as well, on each side of the political spectrum. The Right viewed the effective nationalization of curriculum content standards as an impermissible federal encroachment upon the constitutional rights of the states. The political left saw the new precarity of teachers as a deliberate assault upon one of the largest unions remaining in America at the dawn of the 21st century.

At the close of President Obama's tenure, Congress reauthorized NCLB under a new name, Every Student Succeeds Act (ESSA), and the shaky bipartisan agreement on test-based accountability fractured. The new law required states to use a variety of measures of school performance—including and preponderantly test scores—but also such things as graduation rates, and at least one non-academic metric. The political right hailed this development as a return of state sovereignty over educational matters, while the left bemoaned it for the same reason. As social justice advocate Liz King stated, "the lesson of the civil rights movement and community is that the federal government is the defender of vulnerable children and we are worried that with new state and local authority, vulnerable children are going to be at risk" (Huetteman & Rich, 2015, paragraph 21). At the same time, however, the reality on the ground did not change enough to satisfy the political right. States ceased using the "Common Core State Standards" in large numbers but continued to use the major tests aligned to those standards (Browne, 2015), making the abandonment of the Common Core label more of a branding exercise than a substantive change.

If the left and the right found themselves in large and uncharacteristic agreement over the rationale for standardizing American education on a foundation of routine and rigorous testing, they *also* found themselves in large and uncharacteristic agreement over the failures of that testing to entail the benefits that each side expected. The school choice movement shows this most clearly. The left championed school choice early on primarily because it gave families an alternative to perennial awful neighborhood schools, as Witte (1998) documents of the Milwaukee Voucher Program. Later, in the Obama years, the left's push to increase charter schools was anchored by a new experimentalism, an urge to discover "what works." A competitive marketplace, for Arne Duncan, would reveal the one best way to educate kids that the system could then take to scale. For the right, meanwhile, school choice was both a tool to improve the public schools and a matter of principle. Milton Friedman (1962) proposed an early version of a voucher system partly to force educational institutions to reflect the plural educational values of society, and also because such a system would weed out inefficient or underperforming schools.

None of this worked out as expected, however. NCLB included a provision that allowed students in failing schools to transfer to another school in the district, and on the government's dime, and yet, startlingly, few families took the state up on its offer, apparently preferring to stay with their local schools (Cohn, 2005; Hess & Finn, 2004). The right understood this as reflecting, in racially-coded language, the low-information nature of the families in question (Tyre, 2011). The left saw it more charitably as a governmental failure to make data properly accessible. But in neither case was it politically imaginable that values *other* than test scores mattered to families.

Arne Duncan and Milton Friedman advocated for "school choice," seeking to use competitive dynamics to improve public schooling. However, because they imagined the systemic ideal of public education in different ways, trying to occupy a middle ground that they happened to share ultimately defeated their purposes in coming to agree in the first place. For Duncan, choice was simply a means to an end: competition would cause the (single) best way for education systems to rise out of the chaos *so that* they could be scaled and standardized. Friedman's version of choice, meanwhile, was predicated on an inherent value of pluralism, which resisted scaling entirely. To treat choice as Duncan proposed to do was to miss the point: competition, in Friedman's version, would be much more limited, resulting in the best versions of several kinds of schools, rather than a universally replicable model. Duncan's view simply overlooks the value pluralism that Friedman rightly fastens upon. Friedman's view underestimates the state's interest in ensuring that all children receive an adequate education.

The reality of school choice that emerged, one that pitted schools against one another in competition for student bodies, found itself simultaneously intertwined with state accountability policies. That is, schools were effectively subject to reward and punishment by "clients," to use Principal Rice's term, *and* by the state, simultaneously. All schools were under enormous pressure to avoid state sanctions, especially under NCLB, preventing any school from attempting anything too pedagogically or organizationally daring. Partly because of the research findings that linked high test scores to positive life destinies, the "choices" that families made often significantly aligned with the state's priorities (Chetty et al., 2011). When families exercised choice, that is, they used test scores as a preponderant criterion, which has had the perverse effect of increasing residential and school segregation (Frankenberg, Siegel-Hawley, & Wang, 2010). With Duncan's test scores as the currency of Friedman's market, the resulting system was neither pluralistic enough to realize Friedman's principles nor, for the same reason, *compelling* enough in leveraging choice to create meaningful improvements in schools.

The mention, however, of the middle ground that Duncan and Friedman share shines a light on the contemporary dominance of neoliberalism as a guiding ethos of governance. In particular, Duncan's faith that the market will yield the best candidate for scaling assumes that those exercising school choice will be rational actors according to a specific definition of rationality. For Duncan, the only value on which families could *rationally* choose a school is the school's effect on student learning. Duncan's premise assumes that with equal possession of information, families in pursuit of identical ends will tend to clamor for admission to the same schools, and those are the schools we ought to be imitating. Those identical ends—the maximum improvement in student learning—are signaled in test scores.

The bafflement experienced by policymakers when families refused the state's offer of a transfer under NCLB throws one kind of wrench into this project. The perennial temptation to on-the-ground educators to engage in score inflation of various kinds is another (Aviv, 2014; Koretz, 2017; O'Neil, 2016). This is, one might say, a *rational* response to the stakes of this competition. The state's violence in closing schools and scattering communities that are judged insufficiently rational by these standards is yet another kind of problem for the system (Ewing, 2018). The convergence of ideological commitments around the notion of test-driven educational accountability has therefore enabled 40 years of policy changes on a massive scale, while also underwriting travesties of justice from the perspective of each side of the political aisle. The AIC provides each side of the spectrum sufficient reason to buy in, and that buy-in entails the power to make sweeping changes. Still, the attempt to conduct accountability at the level of the individual family and at the level of the state undercuts the possibility of successfully doing either. Nevertheless, within this enframing of education by the AIC, a consistently expressed consensus is not required for the maintenance of dominant interests, only a consistency that certain potential key issues remain latent issues and that certain interests remain unrecognized.

References

Aviv, R. (2014, July 14). Wrong answer: In an era of high-stakes tests, a struggling school made a shocking choice. *The New Yorker*. Retrieved from https://www.newyorker.com/magazine/2014/07/21/wrong-answer.

Berliner, D. C., & Biddle, B. J. (1996). The manufactured crisis: Myths, fraud, and the attack on America's public schools. *Nassp Bulletin, 80*(576), 119–121.

Booher-Jennings, J. (2005). Below the bubble: "Educational triage" and the Texas accountability system. *American Educational Research Journal, 42*(2), 231–268.

Bost, W. A. (1978). Educational chickens come home to the accountability roost. *The Urban Review, 10*(3), 243–247.

Browne, S. (2015). *Dark matters: On the surveillance of blackness*. Durham, NC: Duke University Press.

Bush, G. W. (2000, July 10). *Text: George W. Bush's speech to the NAACP. The Washington Post*. Retrieved from https://www.washingtonpost.com/wp-srv/onpolitics/elections/bushtext071000.htm.

Chetty, R., Friedman, J. N., & Rockoff, J. E. (2011). *The long-term impacts of teachers: Teacher value-added and student outcomes in adulthood [NBER Working Paper No. 17699]*. National Bureau of Economic Research. Retrieved from https://www.nber.org/papers/w17699.

Chetty, R., Friedman, J. N., & Rockoff, J. E. (2014). Measuring the impacts of teachers II: Teacher value-added and student outcomes in adulthood. *American Economic Review, 104*(9), 2633–2679.

Cohn, C. A. (2005). NCLB implementation challenges: The local superintendent's view. *Peabody Journal of Education, 80*(2), 156–169.

Darling-Hammond, L. (2015). *The flat world and education: How America's commitment to equity will determine our future*. New York, NY: Teachers College Press.

Delpit, L. (1995). *Other people's children: Cultural conflict in the classroom*. New York, NY: The New Press.

Ewing, E. L. (2018). *Ghosts in the schoolyard: Racism and school closings on Chicago's south side*. Chicago, IL: University of Chicago Press.

Frankenberg, E., Siegel-Hawley, G., & Wang, J. (2010). *Choice without equity: Charter school segregation and the need for civil rights standards.* The Civil Rights Project. Retrieved from https://files.eric.ed.gov/fulltext/ED509773.pdf.

Friedman, F. (1970, September 13). The social responsibility of business is to increase its profits. *The New York Times Magazine.* Retrieved from https://www.nytimes.com/1970/09/13/archives/a-friedman-doctrine-the-social-responsibility-of-business-is-to.html.

Friedman, M. (1962). *Capitalism and freedom.* Chicago, IL: University of Chicago Press.

Goldstein, D. (2015). *The teacher wars: A history of America's most embattled profession.* Norwell, MA: Anchor Books.

Hacker, J. (2002). *The divided welfare state.* Cambridge: Cambridge Press.

Hess, F. M., & Finn, C. E., Jr. (2004). Inflating the life rafts of NCLB: Making public school choice and supplemental services work for students in troubled schools. *Phi Delta Kappan, 86*(1), 34–40.

hooks, b. (1994). *Teaching to transgress: Education as the practice of freedom.* London: Routledge.

Huetteman, E., & Rich, M. (2015, December 2). House restores local education control in revising no child left behind. *The New York Times.* Retrieved from https://www.nytimes.com/2015/12/03/us/house-restores-local-education-control-in-revising-no-child-left-behind.html#:~:text=WASHINGTON%20%E2%80%94%20The%20House%20on%20Wednesday,to%20states%20and%20local%20districts.

Kane, T. J., Rockoff, J. E., & Staiger, D. O. (2008). What does certification tell us about teacher effectiveness? Evidence from New York City. *Economics of Education Review, 27*(6), 615–631.

Koretz, D. (2017). *The testing charade: Pretending to make schools better.* Chicago, IL: University of Chicago Press.

Kristof, N. (2012, January 11). The value of teachers. *The New York Times.* Retrieved from https://www.nytimes.com/2012/01/12/opinion/kristof-the-value-of-teachers.html.

Lyman, L. (2000). The Democratic leadership council: An explanation of the organization through an examination of educational policy. *Hinckley Journal of Politics, 2,* 47–54.

McCaffrey, D. F., Sass, T. R., Lockwood, J. R., & Mihaly, K. (2009). The intertemporal variability of teacher effect estimates. *Education Finance and Policy, 4*(4), 572–606.

Moses, M. (2016). *Living with moral disagreement: The enduring controversy about affirmative action.* Chicago, IL: University of Chicago Press.

Murakawa, N. (2014). *The first civil right: How liberals built prison America.* Oxford: Oxford University Press.

O'Connor, B. (2003). *A political history of the American welfare system: When ideas have consequences.* Lanham: Rowman & Littlefield.

O'Neil, C. (2016). *Weapons of math destruction: How big data increases inequality and threatens democracy.* New York, NY: Broadway Books.

Ravitch, D. (2010). *The death and life of the great American school system: How testing and choice are undermining education.* New York, NY: Basic Books.

Rice, I. K. (1978). School structure, competency, and accountability. *NASSP Bulletin, 62*(420), 5–11.

Schoenfeld, H. (2018). *Building the prison state: Race and the politics of mass incarceration.* Chicago, IL: University of Chicago Press.

Skocpol, T. (1996). *Boomerang: Clinton's health security effort and the turn against government in U.S. politics.* New York, NY: W.W. Norton.

Skowronek, S. (1982). *Building a new American state: The expansion of national administrative capacities, 1877-1920*. Cambridge: Cambridge University Press.

Suitts, S. (2019, June 4). *Segregationists, libertarians, and the modern "school choice" movement. Southern Spaces*. Retrieved from https://southernspaces.org/2019/segregationists-libertarians-and-modern-school-choice-movement/.

Tampio, N. (2018). *Common core: National education standards and the threat to democracy*. Baltimore, MD: Johns Hopkins University Press.

Tani, K. (2016). *States of dependency*. Cambridge: Cambridge University Press.

Tyre, P. (2011, September 17). Putting parents in charge. *The New York Times*. Retrieved from https://www.nytimes.com/2011/09/18/opinion/sunday/new-school-trigger-laws-take-parent-engagement-to-a-new-level.html.

The National Commission on Excellence in Education. (1983). *A nation at risk: The imperative for educational reform*. Retrieved from https://edreform.com/wpcontent/uploads/2013/02/A_Nation_At_Risk_1983.pdf.

Valentine, L. D. Jr. (1977). *Prediction of Air Force technical training success from ASVAB and educational background*. Air Force Human Resources Lab. Retrieved from https://apps.dtic.mil/dtic/tr/fulltext/u2/a041735.pdf.

U.S. Department of Education. (2002). *No child left behind, accountability and AYP*. Retrieved from https://www2.ed.gov/admins/lead/account/nclbreference/reference.pdf.

Walker, M. (1996). *The President we deserve: Bill Clinton, his rise, falls, and comebacks*. New York, NY: Crown Publishers.

Weaver, R. K. (2000). *Ending welfare as we know it*. Brookings Institution. Retrieved from https://www.brookings.edu/book/ending-welfare-as-we-know-it/.

Weaver, R. K. (2000). *Ending welfare as we know it*. Washington, DC: Brookings Institution Press.

Weir, M., Olaff, A. S., & Skocpol, T. (1988). *The politics of social policy in the United States*. Princeton, NJ: Princeton Press.

Westbury, I. (1984). A nation at risk. *Journal of Curriculum Studies, 16*(4), 431–445.

U.S. Department of Education. (2009). *Race to the top executive summary*. U.S. Department of Education. Retrieved from https://www2.ed.gov/programs/racetothetop/executive-summary.pdf.

Winfield, A. G. (2007). *Eugenics and education in America: Institutionalized racism and the implications of history, ideology, and memory* (Vol. 18). New York, NY: Peter Lang.

Witte, J. F. (1998). The Milwaukee voucher experiment. *Educational Evaluation and Policy Analysis, 20*(4), 229–251.

4

TESTING FOR PROFIT

Billionaire Boys' Club, Edreformers, and All Matter of Money

A multitude of forces exerts pressure on public education. Specifically, market-driven policies over the past four decades have directly and significantly driven education reform policies and practices. Proponents drive much of these reforms with neoliberal ideology and an agenda determined to transform public domains into private ones. Giroux (2006), Parkison (2015), West (2017), and others explain that neoliberal ideology has dominated American society dating back to the 1970s. A neoliberal ideology maintains an all-encompassing nature to which education is subsumed. Under a shared belief that the free market can self-regulate and government regulations thwart prosperity, neoliberalism casts a wide political tent where both the Republican and Democratic parties find common ground. While neoliberalism has attracted support from both sides of the political aisle, it also has its share of critics. According to Brown (2003),

> Neoliberalism is equated with a radically free market: maximized competition and free trade achieved through economic deregulation, elimination of tariffs, and a range of monetary and social policies favorable to business and indifferent toward poverty, social deracination, cultural decimation, long-term resource depletion, and environmental destruction. (p. 38)

Giroux (2006) also decries neoliberalism focusing on its conception of social—of all relations—as primarily economic in nature and as a destructive representation of how things are rather than a discovery about the true nature of the world:

> Free-market fundamentalism rather than democratic idealism is now the driving force of economics and politics in most of the world. It is a market ideology driven not just by profits but by an ability to reproduce itself with

such success that, to paraphrase Fredric Jameson (1994:xii), it is easier to imagine the end of the world than it is to imagine the end of capitalism, even as it creates vast inequalities and promotes human suffering throughout the globe. (p. 77)

Thus, neoliberalism equates all relations to economic ones; economics is a first philosophy and the most fundamental truth about the world. As the economic trumps the societal, political relationships based on democratic ideals are usurped and even replaced with free-market principles. Dollars function like votes, and progress is measured through profits.

Neoliberalism, Education Reform, and the States

Education is not immune to the impact of neoliberal ideology; in fact, it is an institution that has been severely influenced by forces that support a neoliberal agenda. Brown (2003) argues that "neoliberalism carries a social analysis that, when deployed as a form of governmentality, reaches from the soul of the citizen-subject to education policy to practices of empire" (p. 39). While there have certainly been instances of federal mandates that have been implemented to alleviate inequity and inequality in the system of education, like ordering schools to desegregate based on the U.S. Supreme Court ruling in *Brown v. The Board of Education*, many more recent legislative acts, *No Child Left Behind* (NCLB) and *Race to the Top*, have been driven by proponents aligned with a neoliberal set of principles. Nevertheless, while the federal government has influenced public education, states remain primarily in charge of their educational systems. Yet, states, too, are influenced by and aligned with a neoliberal doctrine. It is essential to recognize the role of the states and their contributions toward market solutions for public schools. According to the 10th amendment of the U.S. Constitution: "The powers not delegated to the United States by the Constitution, nor prohibited by it to the States, are reserved to the States respectively, or to the people" (U.S. Const. amend. X).

Accordingly, all 50 state constitutions include education clauses. Nevertheless, these restrictions have not ebbed the federal government's intrusion into matters of the state. Federal legislation like *Elementary and Secondary Education Act of 1965* (U.S. Department of Education, n.d.-a) and the *Individuals with Disabilities Education Act of 1990* (U.S. Department of Education, n.d.-b) can irresistibly incentivize individual states to comply with federal laws and initiatives through the giving and withholding of funding, mainly in the form of block grants. This relationship functions as a form of new federalism (Ravitch, 2013). Arising out of the *New Deal* legislation and the administrative state (Mayeux & Tani, 2016; Milov, 2019), states are given some autonomy for social and economic experimentation (Brandeis, 1932), but federal funding goes to the states willing to comply with federal policy. From a market perspective, the federal government can also incentivize states to compete with one another for federal resources, like $4.35 billion in grant money for *Race to the Top* funds (U.S. Department of Education, n.d.-c). By constructing the allocation of funding as a competitive endeavor—in which the U.S. Department of Education sets the rules and criteria—the federal government has been able to persuade states into changing their laws in specific ways (e.g., weakening teacher tenure and changing teacher evaluation protocols) while states nominally retain their autonomy. For example, according to the Center for American Progress, when Obama enacted the *Race to the Top* initiative,

> forty states and the District of Columbia eventually applied for funding, and the U.S. Department of Education announced the winners of Phase 1—Delaware and Tennessee—in March 2010. The Department of Education released the names of the Phase 2 winners in August 2010, and they included the District of Columbia, Florida, Georgia, Hawaii, Maryland, Massachusetts, New York, North Carolina, Ohio, and Rhode Island. (Note: Another seven states received RTT Phase 3 grants in December 2011)
>
> *(Boser, 2012, p. 1)*

These states had little choice but to embrace the neoliberal foundations of competition and privatization to receive funding. Colorado is one instance of a state falling prey to the incentivization of *Race to the Top* (RTT). After failing to "win" Phase One RTT funding, competing against Illinois, New Mexico, Oregon, and Wisconsin for $133 million in federal funding, the Colorado State Legislature passed the *Educator Effectiveness Law of 2010.* This law mandated the state to base 50% of teacher and administrator job performance evaluations on student growth (Colorado Department of Education, n.d.) This law includes teachers teaching subjects covered on the state assessment program as well as subjects not assessed on the formal statewide assessment program, such as social studies and the arts. For "core" subjects, like math, both the state assessment and classroom assessments are used in calculating student growth. A school or district may decide what assessments it wants to use in addition to the state assessment to show growth. In other words, different assessments like the *Northwest Evaluation Association Measurement of Academic Progress* (NWEA MAPS) may be used in addition to the state assessment. Enacting legislation like *Educator Effectiveness Law* helped Colorado to eventually "win" $18 million in federal funding from the third and final round of the RTT initiative (U.S. Department of Education, 2014), but that win came with costs. Students would take more standardized assessments, and all public school teachers in Colorado would have their evaluations and tenure status based on the results of the tests (even when they do not teach tested subjects; Colorado Department of Education, 2013). Competing for RTT dollars, especially in states with low levels of public education funding like Colorado (Oliff & Leachman, 2011), may have seemed quite necessary at the time. In hindsight, however, competing for RTT tightened the stranglehold the

Assessment Industrial Complex (AIC) already had on states, teachers, and students. To borrow a line from the Mel Brooks' (1987) comedy *Spaceballs*, if NCLB was taking public schools at warped speed toward neoliberalism, then RTT had us at ludicrous speed in the same direction.

Further, RTT was inherently punitive, focusing more on how to help states and districts utilize high-stakes standardized test scores (i.e., the "objective" data) to sanction and shutter schools rather than improve them and benefit communities. As Ravitch (2013) points out, "the practice of closing schools because of low test scores ha[d] become routine, barely getting notice in the media … in the past, those in charge of school systems were expected to fix troubled schools, not shut them down" (p. 314). So, what happens when a school is shuttered? Often it is replaced with a charter school, or students are enrolled in other schools, sometimes requiring children to travel beyond their local neighborhoods and communities to receive their education. Yet, despite these actions, state and local officials support the closing of schools (Ewing, 2018).

High-Stakes Testing: The Anchor to Which All Education Outcomes Are Tethered

Part of how high-stakes testing and assessments in general anchor education is through the power of a collective of education reformers aligning with a neoliberal agenda. Utilizing rhetoric that reinforces the idea that "greed is good," Edreformers share a socio-political worldview where enterprising individuals, in pursuit of private success, drive a process of invention and innovation that they argue ultimately yield public benefits. These reformers take test scores as the unproblematic evidence of student learning and educational success. As Brown (2003) attests,

> The political sphere, along with every other dimension of contemporary existence, is submitted to an economic rationality; or, put the other way around, not only is the human being configured exhaustively as homo œconomicus, but all dimensions of human life are cast in terms of a market rationality. (p. 40)

Market competition incentivizes local actors to raise test scores, which, for proponents of current education reforms, is the appropriate approach to improving education. Hence, there are the two pieces that are required for Edreformers to pursue their agenda: agreement on a currency (test scores) and agreement on a view of the human as fundamentally motivated to pursue their own maximum benefit (Parkison, 2009). Further, Edreformers rely on the data from testing to legitimize their positions by anchoring all claims, rhetorically, to these assessments. They utilize language to normalize and legitimize the value of tests and the data extracted from them.

Why Edreform?

Education reformers, as Koretz (2017) and others have attested (Petrovic, 2019; Zhao, 2018), are motivated by a variety of intentions and outcomes. Ravitch (2013) argues that these "reformers" (recently, Ravitch (2020) refers to them as "Disruptors") claim to want "excellent education for all; they want great teachers; they want to 'close the achievement gap;' they want innovation and effectiveness; they want the best of everything for everyone" (p. 19). Perhaps many Edreformers' intentions are, in fact, based on their perceived understanding of students' best interests (Parkison, 2015). Regardless, the consequences of education reforms that focus on testing have been disastrous for teachers, students, parents, and society as a whole.

Thomas (2012) points out that education reforms are supported by the political and corporate elite who reinforce their power by using the rhetoric of education reform and accountability to maintain the status quo. Kincheloe (2001) expands on this stating,

> In such an insidious and covert context, power wielders shape our "democratic" schools with little democratic participation. In this political domain, those with the most power dictate purpose…those with the most power are business and corporate leaders and their political allies who in the language of standards specify the types of workers they want. Such specifications…operate to serve the political economic interests of business managers more than the interests of their employees. (p. 12)

Bowles and Gintis (2011) similarly argue that a "system based on free-markets in land and labor and the private ownership of the means of production, if left to itself, would produce a host of undesirable outcomes" (p. 19). Further, "education and state policy are relatively powerless to rectify social problems within a capitalist economy" (p. 20). Thus, Edreformers' rhetoric betrays an underlying reality of the material effects of capitalism and the capacity of the education system to improve the lives of students and the society in which we live. That is, it is disingenuous for proponents of education reform—reform that relies on testing data and the devaluing of students, schools, and communities—to suggest that a particular reform or policy will positively impact society. It is capitalism, "not technology or human nature, [that] is the limiting factor" (Bowles & Gintis, 2011, p. 20). In fact, under the neoliberal order in which capitalism thrives, inequality, in all aspects of society, has widened rather than narrowed (Berman, Ben-Jacob, & Shapira, 2016; Bowles & Gintis, 2011; Fiorentini, 2014).

A clear example of this resulted from the enactment of *No Child Left Behind* (NCLB). As discussed previously, in 2002, NCLB provided a federal mandate that led all states toward the production and/or purchase of standard-based assessments. Even when states developed their assessments, they often outsource the labor to large companies at a cost to the states engaging in these practices. In fact, before the passage of NCLB, the testing industry had more than four decades of large profit margins (Hoffman, Assaf, & Paris, 2001). Before the 2000 U.S. Presidential election, the *Wall Street Journal* identified McGraw-Hill, Houghton-Mifflin, and Harcourt as "Bush stocks" because these publishing companies were especially poised to profit from the expanding assessment market if George W. Bush was elected U.S. President. After becoming President, the "Bush stocks" rose in both profit and political influence (Metcalf, 2002). For example, Harold McGraw III, a long-time Bush family friend and CEO of McGraw-Hill, was appointed to Bush's transition team. John Negroponte left his position as McGraw-Hill's executive vice president for global markets to accept an appointment as ambassador to the United Nations. Rod Paige, former Houston Independent School District Superintendent, and McGraw-Hill insider was appointed U.S. Secretary of Education. The McGraw-Hill Company was undoubtedly tied to the George W. Bush presidency.

Mandating public-school accountability via standardized assessments was considered one of George W. Bush's crowning achievements during his time as Governor of Texas (Moore & Slater, 2011). Creating a federal law to ensure public school accountability through mandating standardized testing befitted President Bush's first major domestic focus and resulted in the bipartisan passage of NCLB. Five years after NCLB became law, a PBS investigation found four companies, Harcourt Educational Measurement, CTB McGraw-Hill, Riverside Publishing (a company owned by Houghton Mifflin), and NCS Pearson, were producing 96% of state standardized assessments associated with NCLB, and billions of dollars were annually allocated from federal and state taxes to purchase and administer these standardized assessments. The "Bush stocks" were indeed paying off (Leistyna, 2007).

Drilling Deeper: Other Education Reform Movements

Focusing on conservatism and education, Petrovic (2019) decries the construction of students in "problematic ways" (p. 5). He pointedly names several movements that comprise the conservative modernization movement (a phrase coined by Michael Apple). According to Petrovic (2019), the conservative modernization movement includes "conservatism, neoconservatism, and authoritarian populism" (p. 4). Moreover, those agents that function within this collective exert tremendous influence on educational policy and reform. Petrovic (2019) considers neoliberalism to be the "dominant movement" (p. 5) that grounds this alliance and anchors test scores to the movement's outcomes:

> Test scores stand in for student identity, linked together to grant a determination for what a student is (a good student, a high/low-achieving student, etc.); teachers are applauded or reprimanded for the degree to which their students statistically improve; schools are deemed

successful or "failing" based on the historical trajectory of student outcome measures; the U.S. educational system is shown to be "falling behind" other countries (namely Japan and Germany in science and math). (p. 5)

As Petrovic notes, student identity is only a test score. The consequence of this reality is that test scores anchor the possibilities of student identity in place, restricting their movement. However, while Petrovic argues that the failure of schools is in "student outcome measures," in reality, the real damage lies in our inability to imagine any piece of the education puzzle (including outcomes, student identity, teaching practices, human motivation, etc.) in a way that does not ultimately return the focus to test scores (Knoester & Parkison, 2017). Koretz (2017) too links these outcomes to an "adherence to a normative neoliberal logic ..." (p. 5) that utilizes test scores in all their forms to anchor our understanding of what it means to say that not only a school is succeeding or failing, but also the society at large.

Overarchingly, it is the neoliberal movement that limits our understanding of what is possible in education and our society through discourse that limits our capacity to understand a different vision of education. NCLB is a clear example of the translation of an ideological movement on a social institution. As Ross and Gibson (2007) attest in the introduction to their edited text, *Neoliberalism and Education Reform,* "NCLB is part of the global and national neoliberal agenda and intensifies the war on youth of color. NCLB is rooted in global competition over markets and investments and by cultural struggles over race, ethnicity, language, and national identity" (p. 10). Lipman (2006), who addresses NCLB in her chapter in the text, argues that "NCLB policies and the discourse surrounding them become a 'discourse policy' directed to society as a whole, defining educational problems and their solutions so as to limit the possibilities we have of thinking and acting otherwise" (p. 10). The power of education reformers to utilize rhetoric to suggest that such reforms will affect positive social change could only be possible if the system in which education functions accounted for and addressed the structural and systemic inequities and inequalities that govern the system. However, instead of Edreformers tackling or even admitting to these structural issues, their strategies and discourse reduce public resistance by encouraging business leaders to place social accountability on the individual rather than the community, consequently shifting the relationship between community and the individual (Hursh, 2007).

These tactics play out in school districts across the country where teachers, students, and parents become the focus of responsibility for student learning outcomes rather than the State or powerful stakeholders controlling the system. Whether through policy, legislation, and/or explicit media, their messaging characterizes the failure of schools as the failure of the individual (e.g., the teacher, the student, the parent; Saltman, 2016). Testing is the mechanism that allows those in power to anchor their discursive framing of the problem. That is, instead of focusing on the inequities (e.g., poverty, bias test-item questions) as contributable to the causes of "failure," Edreformers utilize language that shifts the blame and responsibility to those who have little influence over these determinants.

In 2013, Diane Ravitch published a text entitled *Reign of Error: The Hoax of the Privatization Movement and the Danger to America's Public Schools* (Ravitch, 2013). In this text, she states,

> The "reformers" say they want excellent education for all; they want great teachers; they want to "close the achievement gap;" they want innovation and effectiveness; they want the best of everything for everyone. They pursue these universally admired goals by privatizing education, lowering the qualifications for future teachers, replacing teachers with technology, increasing class sizes, endorsing for-profit organizations to manage schools, using carrots and sticks to motivate teachers and elevating standardized test scores as the ultimate measure of education quality. (p. 19)

There is an increasing number of avenues by which education reform has been occurring in the United States over the past few decades. And as stated, these reform efforts harken back to Milton Friedman (1962, 1970), *A Nation at Risk*, NCLB, and other education reform legislation that have systematically limited the purpose and function of education. Lipman (2006) states,

> Beginning with A Nation at Risk (National Commission, 1983) and other education reform manifestos of the 1980s, there has been a steady push for standards, accountability, and regulation of schools, teachers, and students and an explicit linkage of corporate interests with educational practices and goals. (p. 35)

Lipman further points out that the "rhetoric of efficiency and performance standards" (p. 35) has shifted education policy to reshape and limit the purpose of education that focuses on serving the labor market (Parkison, 2015). The development and implementation of the Common Core State Standards (CCSS) is partly a result of what began with NCLB pressure to hold states, districts, teachers, and students accountable for student achievement. Since its publication in 2010, the CCSS has focused on standards, accountability, and testing, all in a stated effort to lead students to college or career readiness. As stated on its website, "The Common Core State Standards are a clear set of shared goals and expectations for the knowledge and skills students need in English language arts and mathematics at each grade level so they can be prepared to succeed in college, career, and life" (Common Core State Standards Initiative, n.d., paragraph 8). Thus, at least one outcome of NCLB resulted in the CCSS, standards that reduce the purpose of education to basic market fundamentals and rely on the testing data to interpret the results. None of this can occur without anchoring these standards to a high-stakes test and then justifying the test, with the need to hold teachers and students "accountable" to the outcomes of success (or failure) as measured by these tests (hence, the stakes).

Seeing the Reality from The Rhetoric

These accountability measures supposedly indicate that reform policies are addressing the "problem" of failing schools. As Lipman (2006) points out,

> Tough accountability measures suggest that something is finally being done to make sure that all children can read and do math, with schools, educators, and students held accountable for results. Tying educational programs to accountability for results (test scores) resonates with the often repeated idea that schools have not improved despite a proliferation of reforms. (p. 36)

It is curious how, despite the proliferation of education reforms implemented since the enactment of NCLB, the oft-repeated message concerning education is that students are still performing poorly in large numbers. As mentioned in Chapter 1, the recent release of NAEP scores reinvigorates Edreformers' argument that education is failing to prepare students to be prepared for college and careers. As the Center for Education Reform (CER), a conservative organization that promotes education reform, remarked on their website:

> Last year, on the 35th anniversary of the release of *A Nation at Risk* the latest NAEP scores were yet again a sobering reminder that far too many children and young adults are not well educated, prepared to enter college or the workforce, and ultimately, able to achieve the level of prosperity this nation offers and makes possible for every citizen.
>
> *(Center for Education Reform, n.d., paragraph 8)*

Yet, as the Hechinger Report, another education news outlet, commented regarding the 2019 NAEP score results,

> Leslie Muldoon, executive director of the National Assessment Governing Board, which jointly oversees the test along with NCES, called the bleak score report "frustrating and difficult to understand" because of all the efforts to improve education. Those include holding schools and teachers accountable for student performance, the introduction of more rigorous Common Core standards, the increased use of education technology and the expansion of charter schools.
>
> *(Barshay, 2019, paragraph 5)*

Despite the number of education reforms that focus on school choice, standards, testing, and accountability, there is a myriad of reasons for school children's "poor" academic performance other than the reforms that have been implemented over the past two decades. In an article published in *Education Next*, an outlet supporting corporate education reform policies, Kress argues that there are several reasons for the inadequate NAEP results. Sandy Kress, a senior education adviser to President George W. Bush, stated,

> As I said in my preview, this picture is in no way surprising. We've done nothing this decade that should have moved the dial. We have a national policy called Every Student Succeeds [ESSA], yet there's really nothing in that policy that demands or even incentivizes changes in the status quo that would likely yield success.
>
> *(NAEP Report Card, n.d., paragraph 13)*

It is interesting how Kress blames ESSA, only signed into law in December of 2015, approximately five years ago (how long does it take for policy to effect change in a system?) for the poor NAEP results but not the 13 years of NCLBs punitive policies. On the same webpage, Paul Peterson, a senior fellow at the Hoover Institution, a right-wing, conservative think tank, offered an even more confusing comment: "clearly, now is the time to put accountability policy back on the nation's educational agenda" (NAEP Report Card, n.d., paragraph 32).

> Exactly when was accountability for student outcomes taken off the national agenda? Michael Petrilli adds to the neo-conservative chorus of interpretations of NAEPs "dismal" test scores: It's the troubling truth that America's academic progress as a whole remains extremely disappointing. That it doesn't have to be that way is also true, however, as illustrated by the handful of states and districts that are making notable gains. Let us follow their lead.
>
> *(NAEP Report Card, n.d., paragraph 38)*

Pertrilli is the President of the right-wing neo-conservative Thomas B. Fordham Institute, where demonizing public education is a sport. Petrilli is long known as an advocate for education reform in the United States. Nevertheless, when all of the reform efforts he has supported for nearly two decades leads to disappointing NAEP results, he shifts his tone to one of positivity stating:

> A few jurisdictions bucked the overall trends and showed improvement. Washington, D.C., deserves much of the attention, given its ability to demonstrate sustained and significant progress over time, and its decade-plus commitment to fundamental reform. Yet even D.C. comes with a demographic asterisk, given the rapidly changing population of the nation's capital. It's also true that, in many ways, the Great Recession skipped D.C.; let me encourage analysts in coming days to figure out how much credit

should go to the schools and how much belongs to economic and social conditions.

(NAEP Report Card, n.d., paragraph 34)

Understandably, Petrilli focuses on some of the positive NAEP results and shifts the focus to the economy by discussing Kindergartners who would have been affected by the Great Recession. This is his rhetorical attempt to shift attention and responsibility for the "failure" of schools to the economy and away from nearly two decades of education reforms that focus on testing and accountability. In analyzing the rhetoric and discourse of proponents of education reform, it is challenging to counteract the message. As Lipman and other scholars attest, all these reforms are grounded in ideology and belief that the purpose of education is to develop workers to support and expand the economy. However, to maintain the appearance of objectivity, fairness, and equity, proponents of reform continue to focus on and utilize the data from testing to argue for accountability and more testing, even when that data indicates that the very same solution was a failure.

Should We All Be Accountable or Just Some of Us?

There is an interesting yet dichotomous argument often put forth by Edreformers concerning accountability. On the one hand, proponents of education reform argue that districts, schools, teachers, and students must be held accountable to meet the outcomes set forth by the state to demonstrate that students are in fact learning and to monitor when schools are failing. However, not all accountability requirements seem to be applicable in all educational contexts. When it comes to charter schools, for example, many proponents of charters do not accept the same set of accountability demands arguing that they are erroneous, heavy-handed, and undermining of the "intent" of the mission of charter schools. As Lewis (2018) notes, "State and local policies, rules, and guidance continue to undermine the flexibility to innovate, making many charter schools across the country nothing more than a charter school in name only" (paragraph 8). Irrespective of the veracity of this claim across charter schools nationwide, Lewis' point that for charters to be successful implies that they should be freed from the restrictions of oversight and accountability speaks to a certain hypocrisy among some Edreformers. While a discussion of whether or not, or the degree to which, charter schools are held accountable is beyond the scope of this chapter, the point is that many education reformers want to apply an accountability metric to traditional public schools that they do not want simultaneously to apply to schools accepting vouchers, charters, etc. In fact, as one former executive vice president of the Georgia Charter Schools Association stated, "Accountability matters. Failing to recognize appropriate accountability in the charter sector makes the sector hypocritical toward the standards we say we live by" (Lewis, 2018, paragraph 23). Hypocrisy regarding accountability seems to be an issue with many Edreformers. There are many types of education reforms and a broad spectrum of Edreformers who dedicate their time, energy, and wealth to effecting change in the system of public education in the United States and abroad. But when it comes to being held accountable for how they apply their wealth to impact change, quite often, there is no accountability. Yet, Edreformers routinely attempt to influence policy and shift the rhetoric of accountability to focus on the failure of traditional public schools to close the academic achievement gap (Lipman, 2006; Ravitch, 2013).

This is another iteration of how Edreformers apply accountability mechanisms to traditional public schools to further their neoliberal agenda. They demonstrate "failure" via testing data but ignore other data demonstrating how public schools are defunded and deprived of needed resources, simultaneously arguing the notion of competition and equity to ground their position. For example, on the website of Dropout Nation, it states that the contributing writers to the website illuminate issues through "the objective and honest use of data" (Dropout Nation, n.d., paragraph 1). On a different webpage, the focus is on the supposed hypocrisy of the American Federation of Teachers (AFT) and its leader Randi Weingarten who advocates for restrictions on charter school growth nationwide. In his analysis, Biddle (2015) accuses Weingarten, The Center for Popular Democracy, and In the Public Interest (both left-wing organizations), of demanding that states require an impact analysis to determine the effect that the opening of new charters will have on the traditional public schools within a district. He then argues that these re-commendations would serve Weingarten's and AFTs interests and limit educational choices for parents instead of providing "high-quality schools to children, especially those from poor and minority households who need it the most" (paragraph 4). First, Dropout Nation's use of rhetoric that describes data as "objective and honest" is deceiving because the "data" they refer to is itself often invalid and unreliable (Knoester & Au, 2015; Koretz, 2017). Second, feigning to understand the needs of children from poor and minority households demonstrates how Edreformers' focus is on promoting a neoliberal agenda rather than focusing on how testing and other education reforms, such as the expansion of charter schools, have undermined communities of color and poverty (Kendi, 2016; Ravitch, 2013). By his own admission, Biddle (2015) states,

> Certainly, the charter school movement needs to be concerned about bad operators whose financial and academic malfeasance (along with mere incompetence in improving student achievement) can cast the entire sector and the school reform movement as whole in a bad light. This includes shutting down authorizers who are allowing failing charter operators and their schools to remain in business long after it is clear that they're not making the grade. (paragraph 3)

Notice how the language utilized in this context shifts to an innocuous tone (they need only be "concerned" rather than "alarmed"), but more interesting is the focus, again, on testing. When Edreformers refer to student achievement, they are referring to the outcomes of standardized testing (Strong, Silver, & Perini, 2001; Walberg, 2010). And while Biddle (2015) acknowledges the need to shut down poorly operated charter schools, his focus remains on critiquing those pushing against the expansion of charters rather than explaining why bad operators are, in the first place, allowed to continue running their failing charter schools with impunity. Additionally, Biddle (2015) cites studies from the Rand Corp, and Knowledge is Power Program (KIPP; a charter school conglomerate) to demonstrate that charters are more successful (again, academically, and again, basing this notion of success on test scores) than traditional public schools. Yet, multiple studies report that only a small number of students attending charter schools outperform students who attend traditional public schools and that, often, students attending charter schools frequently perform worse, in particular in math (CREDO, n.d.). Moreover, KIPP schools are often critiqued for their rigid emphasis on discipline, test scores, high rate of teacher burnout, and high rate of student attrition (Abundis, Crego-Emley, Baker, & Lema, 2017).

The Intertwining of Accountability, Power, and Wealth

Another alarming issue that needs to be addressed when drilling more in-depth into the impact of education reform movements is the relationship between accountability and those who utilize their wealth and status to impact change in education and society. One popular approach currently to applying one's wealth to transform systems is through a charitable foundation. As Posner (2006) contends, we should all be quite wary of this approach:

> A perpetual charitable foundation, however, is a completely irresponsible institution, answerable to nobody. It competes neither in capital markets nor in product markets…and, unlike a hereditary monarch whom such a foundation otherwise resembles, it is subject to no political controls either. It is not even subject to benchmark competition…The puzzle for economics is why these foundations are not total scandals. (paragraph 1)

Posner's argument provides a warning, in particular to those of us in the education sector who recognize the impact charitable organizations and wealthy philanthropists have on education reform. As Posner points out, and as Ravitch and others have recognized, there is no accountability mechanism for grant-making foundations. Further, given that a 2011 Gallup poll revealed that Americans consider Bill Gates and Warren Buffet (both have influential foundations of their own) "among the ten most admired Americans" (Reich, 2013, paragraph 4), one might inquire what the role of charitable foundations and wealthy philanthropists are in a democratic society "committed, at least in principle, to the equality of citizens" (Reich, 2013, paragraph 5). Reich (2013) also points out,

> Foundations, in contrast, do not sell goods and face no marketplace competitors. Instead of selling anything, foundations give money to other organizations. Don't like the grant-making decisions of a foundation? Tough, there's nothing to buy, no investors to hold them accountable. (paragraph 10)

Since there is no accountability to the stakeholders impacted by the decisions and outcomes of the work of the foundations, these institutions wield great power with impunity. Moreover, they are tax-subsidized; that is, the money endowed to a non-profit philanthropic organization is not taxed, so they should be held publicly accountable. Reich (2013) states, "the fact remains that foundations are partly the product of public subsidies. They are created voluntarily, but they result in a loss of funds that would otherwise be tax revenue" (paragraph 24). Furthermore, this is at a significant cost to the American taxpayer, "In 2011 tax subsidies for charitable giving cost the U.S. Treasury an estimated $53.7 billion" (Reich, 2013, paragraph 24). Thus, not only are the mega-wealthy able to shield their money from being taxed, they can utilize their money to advance their ideological agenda without any accountability.

Diane Ravitch (2013, 2020), Mercedes Schneider (2015), and other progressive scholars have written extensively about billionaires who utilize their wealth to create educational change and pursue outcomes they deem appropriate for the general public. Often billionaire Edreformers include Bill and Melinda Gates, Eli and Edyth Broad, and the Walton family. For example, in 2011, in a *Dissent* magazine article entitled "Got Dough? How Billionaires Rule Our Schools," Barkan pointed out that hundreds of private philanthropies together spend almost $4 billion annually to support or transform K–12 education, but three funders—the Bill and Melinda Gates Foundation, the Eli and Edythe Broad (rhymes with road) Foundation, and the Walton Family Foundation—working in sync, command the field. (paragraph 2). Since 2011, the impact on education reform of the "Gates-Broad-Walton triumvirate" (Barkan, 2011, paragraph 2) has not abated. Thus, in debating whether or not to continue in this tradition of critiquing what Ravitch (2013) calls "the Billionaire Boys Club," we determined that we would address and analyze the ongoing actions of these powerful stakeholders and their foundations given the impact billionaires wealth still has on public education. Grounding this analysis in both the past and current context, readers can understand the power those with seemingly endless wealth have in shaping the outcomes of the lives of others. A consistent dilemma within the educational context is the level of awareness that these extremely powerful eduphilanthropist and Edreformers have on the hegemonic narrative generated by the AIC. The ubiquitous language and political economy of standardized testing enframe the vision and efforts of these power brokers in education, leaving some options as "obvious" choices for action and others as unrecognizable.

Money Runs the Show

Pointing out that people with wealth, status, and power use their foundations to impact change seems rather obvious, perhaps even pointless, until one realizes that being entirely unaccountable for their advocacy work through their foundations, irrespective of their intentions, is undemocratic, and perhaps even anti-democratic and racist (Kendi, 2019). Moreover, standardized tests are the anchor that grounds their rhetoric and "advocacy" in a distorted interpretation of reality informed by a neoliberal lens. Without the data from the "objective and valid" high-stakes and other standardized tests, their arguments would lack the appearance of validity and a justification for their being the saviors of poor, needy kids. In other words, the rhetoric of the AIC, the continuous and ubiquitous narrative of standardization, testing, and accountability, oblige even the powerbrokers to legitimate their efforts in the language of the AIC. This narrative is unquestioned. Using "objective and valid" data from high-stakes testing for accountability and measures of opportunity gaps has become banal within education.

As we have discussed throughout this chapter, the ultra-wealthy are committed to certain neoliberal ideologies that privilege market choice, competition, and quantitative accountability (but only for *others,* not those who are privileged). This commitment blinds them to alternate forms and interpretations of evidence (e.g., testing data, poor academic outcomes for many students in charter schools and those using vouchers). Shifting their perspectives could offer much-needed insight that their choices and behaviors are inadequate to address what they perceive are problems in public education. Further, their determination to blindly impose their power on others, immunes them to alternative strategies of social organization that could improve the outcomes of the very people they claim to want to help.

Thus, an examination of the evidence that may convince Edreformers, and in particular those billionaires and other "philanthropists" committed to reforming education in the name of addressing poverty and opportunity, could begin with a fundamental analysis of the failures and persistence of these proponents of education reform. Given their approach to education reform is often undemocratic, and even racist, one might ask, "what are the impacts of an anti-democratic, racist political ideology as it concerns education?" And, "how are the uber-wealthy impinging on the rights of others from having access to high-quality, equitable and purposeful educational experiences that would advance them in society? The next section begins to tackle these challenging but significant questions.

How Edreformers Wield Their Power

On her blog, Mercedes Schneider (2019) posted from a piece in *The Hill* about Gates' desire to start a nonprofit lobbying organization. Gangitano (2019) cites Rob Nabors, Obama's former director of legislative affairs, saying,

Bill and Melinda have been interested in improving the outcome of the poorest in society both here in the United States and abroad for a very long time, Nabors told The Hill. I think recently Bill and Melinda have asked the question, "Is there more that we can be doing, especially here in the United States?" (paragraph 4)

There are several significant aspects to this comment: First, Billionaires like the Gates presume that given their wealth and status, they will serve a paternal role and determine what are considered societal ills. Given their power, they claim to be the people responsible and capable of solving these "problems" irrespective of the adverse effects, historically, they have had on the people they portend to help. The Gates Foundation supported many failed attempts at school reform. Recall their failed initiative with small schools (Schneider, 2019; Strauss, 2014), where the Gates Foundation spent over $2 billion breaking down large high schools into smaller ones. As Schneider (2019) recently pointed out:

Gates Foundation grants have supported some worthwhile education efforts, but its biggest pushes in the past decades have not succeeded as planned. The foundation began its first big effort in this realm 20 years ago with what it said was a $650 million investment to divide big, failing high schools into smaller schools, on the theory that smaller schools worked better. (paragraph 13)

In many ways, the CCSS, another initiative supported by Gates, has struggled as well. A discussion of the issues with the CCSS is beyond the scope of this chapter, but as Strauss (2019) points out, "After that, the foundation funded development, implementation, and promotion of the Common Core and worked with Duncan to keep it alive despite backlash" (paragraph 14). Tying teacher evaluations to students' test scores (Koretz, 2017; Schneider, 2019) has been another problematic initiative supported by Gates. While we address this in more depth in Chapter 5, studies support that these evaluation systems have had numerous negative impacts on students, teachers, and schools (Croft, Roberts, & Stenhouse, 2015; Koretz, 2017; Paufler, 2018).

Additionally, each of these initiatives has had and continues to negatively impact the communities in which the schools serve their students. Instead of utilizing grant funding to address issues of poverty directly, mental health in schools, etc., the Gates' Foundation, by supporting small school initiatives, and by Bill Gates own admission, failed at school reform and wasted hundreds of millions of dollars in the process (Schneider, 2019). Even if we acknowledge that Bill Gates' attempts at school reform are his approach to alleviating poverty in the United States, given their repeated failures, when should he be held accountable for the damage his reforms have done to students' and teachers' lives? Either these outcomes were unintentional, and therefore Gates is irresponsible, or they were intentional, which makes him immoral.

Second, despite their consistency in failing at school reform, Bill and Melinda Gates, as Strauss (2019) states, "don't give up" (paragraph 1). As mentioned previously, currently they are utilizing their wealth and power to launch the Gates Policy Initiative, a lobbying organization, whose focus will be "global health, global development, U.S. education and outcomes for black, Latino and rural students specifically, and efforts to move people from poverty to employment" (Gangitano, 2019, paragraph 2). This raises several questions: how will the people they intend to serve feel about and interpret Gates' largess? What power do Blacks, Latinos, and rural students have in determining their outcomes in the face of Gates' imposition on their lives? In fact, in 2014, Ruth Rodriguez of the Save Our Schools Steering Committee and National United Opt-Out administrator developed a blog solely dedicated to teachers' letters to Bill Gates. In one such letter, she inquired,

> So here is a challenge for you, if indeed you are sincere that the reforms you are proposing for our children are the answer, why not try these reforms with the schools that educate the children of the rich and politically influential? Why not take the children in the schools where you, the President [Obama] and the rich send their children; trade places with the children in the schools of the poor, where your education experiments are being implemented.
>
> *(Rodriguez, 2014, paragraph 7)*

It is worth mentioning that employment as a cure for poverty, such as the Gates Foundation is proposing, was created by the Heritage Foundation as a means of tearing down the new deal welfare state via propagating the "dependency thesis" (Medvetz, 2012). As previously discussed, part of a neoliberal ideology supports the belief that the individual, not society, is totally and entirely responsible for their outcomes. Structural and systemic inequities, the impact of unfettered capitalism and free markets, and other societal issues seem to play no part in neoliberal ideology. Yet, their agenda negatively impacts the lives of individuals, in particular people of color and in poverty.

Similar to Bill and Melinda Gates, Eli and Edythe Broad have committed millions of their personal wealth to education reform. Their attempts at reforming education have not gone unnoticed by teachers, administrators, students, and parents who support public schools. According to the Center for Media and Democracy's PRWatch Editors (2018)

> …thousands of teachers, students, and other public school supporters marched in downtown Los Angeles to the Broad Museum to protest billionaires such as Eli Broad that fund the growth of charter schools, many of which are not unionized and divert students from district schools. (paragraph 1)

Broad and other wealthy donors who support the privatization of public schools contributed $41 million to support Marshall Tuck, the California state super-intendent of public instruction in 2018. Some readers may wonder what the issue is with Eli Broad (or any billionaire) funding a campaign election for someone who represents his interests in an election. One may also question what the relationship is between Broad and Marshall Tuck concerning Broad's agenda for public education. We return later to respond to the first issue, but the second is clearly outlined on the Broad Center website: Tuck was a Broad Resident from 2004 to 2006 and has earned a Bachelors of Arts in Political Science from UCLA and an MBA from Harvard Business School (Broadcenter, n.d.-a). Wikipedia describes Tuck as "an American venture capital investor, educator, and politician" (Broadcenter, n.d.-a), but he is also a self-proclaimed Democrat belonging to the Democratic party. As discussed previously, when billionaires utilize their wealth to control the outcomes of elections, public spending, etc., that is inherently undemocratic. As stated on the website, Institute for Democratic Education in America, our society is "based on participation, empowerment, and democracy" (Bennis, n.d., paragraph 1), or so we would like to believe. Thus, shouldn't our elections, which are part of our demo-cratic institutions, align with democratic principles? Shouldn't they be fair, em-powering, and democratic as well? Perhaps today, given the Supreme Court case of Citizen's United vs. Federal Election Committee, where the majority opinion de-termined that the free speech of corporations is more significant than protecting Americans from the power of special interest groups and lobbyists, many no longer question when those with money and power attempt to control the public sphere. For those who still believe in the importance of protecting democratic institutions, Broad's attempt to control the outcome of a state's election for state superintendent represents an abuse of power, and it is anti-democratic. One may think it ironic that Tuck, who ran twice for the position, ran as a Democrat. But voters were not fooled; he lost the race in 2014, despite millions in campaign costs that were spent between Tuck and his adversary Tom Torlakson. As Myers (2018) remarks,

> Some $30 million was spent in the war between bitter education rivals, each convinced it has the better way—and the better candidate—to fix what's broken in state education policy. On one side is a consortium of wealthy backers of charter schools; on the other, powerful teachers' unions. (paragraph 3–4)

In 2018, Tuck again ran for the position and lost to Tony Thurmond. Thurmond, also a Democrat, relinquished his position as an Assemblyman in the Bay Area to run for the position. Further, several wealthy donors contributed to Tuck's campaign, including Eli Broad, members of the Walton family, and Netflix CEO, Reed Hastings. Broad is a rabid supporter of charter schools and claims, like Gates, the Koch brothers, and other Edreformers, that traditional public school education is failing. He insists "that spending public money on privately managed charter or voucher schools is the path to redemption" (PRWatch Editors, 2018, paragraph 4). Broad and other mega-billionaires have spent "hundreds of millions of dollars on education think tank "research" and charter schools, shaping current trends in what they call education reform" (PRWatch Editors, 2018, paragraph 4). And again, he is not alone. According to an article entitled "Eli Broad and the End of Public Education as We Know It," published in 2015, Broad produced a 44-page proposal that outlines plans to shift half of LAUSDs extant public schools to charter schools. In his report, Broad contends that charter schools and their students outperform traditional public school students on standardized tests. However, even the LA School Report, a pro-education reform publication, questions Broad's claims:

> But when all factors are considered, there is little conclusive evidence in the report outlining the expansion plans that shows big investments in charters always—or evenly routinely—achieve consistent academic improvements, raising an important question: Just what can Broad and other foundations promise for an investment of nearly half a billion dollars in an expansion effort that would dramatically change the nation's second-largest school district?
>
> *(Clough, 2015, paragraph 2)*

Despite the veracity, or the lack thereof, of claims made for or against charter or traditional public schools, it is the high-stakes tests that are used to manipulate and support the arguments. Broad, being an influential and powerful stakeholder in Los Angeles, wields that power by manipulating and cherry-picking data sources to support his agenda of the expansion of charter schools. They can use their wealth, unchecked, to determine how the public perceives public education. But as Posner (2006) points out in the quote cited earlier in the chapter, people like Broad, Gates, and the Waltons have unfettered power via their money and foundations to upend public education and to pursue their ideological agenda with little scrutiny and impunity. Those that are impacted by their decision making are the ones harmed (or benefitting) from their "largesse" and lack the money, power, and seemingly endless resources of billionaires, thus making it difficult to challenge and defeat them. Also, it is important to remember that those with vast wealth are not held accountable for the outcomes of their behaviors. Even when they fail, like Gates' many education reform failures, they pivot, shift their rhetoric, and try again.

Educational Leadership Development: Cartel Style

The goals and objectives of many of the education reforms billionaires and other wealthy philanthropists have sought to achieve and continue to advocate for have demonstrably failed to meet their stated expectations despite the vast sums of money they have committed to these endeavors. Hence, one is left to ponder what motivates these individuals and foundations to continue their quest to "improve public education." To understand these motives, one must look beyond the individual to see the vast interconnected network of beneficiaries. Jeffrey Bryant, in his article entitled "How Billionaire Charter School Funders Corrupted the School Leadership Pipeline" comments that Eli Broad and the Broad Foundation have influenced and shaped school leadership across the nation via the leadership programs offered at the Broad Center. Bryant (2019) summarizes an interview with Thomas Pedroni, an associate professor of curriculum studies at Wayne State University.

> According to Pedroni, the school leadership network, especially in large, urban school districts, wields a cartel-like influence that seeks to wrestle school governance away from democratically elected school boards and outsource district management to private contractors, often in the ed-tech industry. These businesses frequently have close associations with colleagues in school reform circles that are directly connected to the Broad network or seek the network's favor. (paragraph 10)

According to the Broad Center's website, there are programs that "cultivate public education leaders" (Broadcenter, n.d.-b, paragraph 1). The two programs include The Broad Academy and The Broad Residency in Urban Education. The website of the former states that the program "brings together game-changing system leaders who develop innovative strategies to tackle some of urban public education's greatest needs" (Broadcenter, n.d.-b, paragraph 4). Whereas the website of the latter states,

> The Broad Residency in Urban Education provides the opportunity for outstanding management professionals to apply their skills and knowledge to meet the challenges faced by urban public-school systems. Whether you've worked in education or not, our two-year program is designed to help you grow professionally as you create positive, lasting impact on behalf of students and communities.
>
> *(Broadcenter, n.d.-b, paragraph 2)*

As Bryant (2019) points out, this rhetoric seems positive and impactful. He notes that "practitioners of the reform creed tend to wrap their management practices in the rhetoric of being 'about kids,' with promises to promote 'equity' and 'student-centered learning'" (paragraph 20). The second program recently partnered with the Yale School of Management. The Eli and Edythe Broad foundation donated a $100 million gift "to develop innovative teaching and research programs devoted to strengthening the leadership of America's public-school systems" (Yale School of Management, 2019, paragraph 2). After completing the program, graduates are strategically placed in powerful positions to reform and shift schools in their system that resemble a corporatist approach to management.

Once in place, Broadies, as they are often referred to, act more corporate and "adopt a corporate language infused with business principles such as resource maximization, market competition, and getting a return on education investment" (Bryant, 2019, paragraph 20). The outsized influence of the Broad Center programs has reshaped what educational leadership looks like across the country. As Bryant (2019) argues, despite the waning influence of some education reforms, what Broad has and continues to accomplish in education leadership, will perhaps remain: "not because it has proven to help turn around troubled schools, but because it's turned school leadership into a profession that does what corporations often do best: advance personal careers and help create higher profits for private enterprises" (paragraph 24).

None of this is possible without homing in on and valuing the data derived from standardized testing. Gates, Broad, and other venture philanthropists frame the rhetoric of accountability on a narrative of failure, and their role, according to them, is to improve educational outcomes, those outcomes being measured by the standardized tests. As noted previously, these tests are constructed and dominated by mega-corporations like Pearson, McGraw-Hill, and others, all of who profit tremendously from the accountability regime. As Broad crowed after the election of President Obama:

> With an agenda that echoes our decade of investments—charter schools, performance pay for teachers, accountability, expanded learning time, and national standards—the Obama administration is poised to cultivate and bring to fruition the seeds we and other reformers have planted.
>
> *(Beder, n.d., paragraph 5)*

Those seeds were rotten, and from them, nothing positive has grown or been cultivated to help the students Edreformers have claimed they would benefit.

Edreformers: Neither Evil nor Stupid, Just Plain Wrong

As demonstrated, billionaires like Broad, Gates, and others utilize their unfathomable wealth to influence and shape societal outcomes in significant and unaccountable ways, often cloaking their benevolence as sacrificial and of absolute necessity to save a public good. Perhaps none of the people, and the foundations and organizations they have developed, seek to destroy public education explicitly. They spend an incredible amount of resources and time trying to "fix" what they incessantly argue is broken. Even when the evidence indicates that the policies, solutions, and strategies they support often do more harm than good, and consequently are the cause of so many failures in public education, they will persist with their agendas.

But if Edreformers, and particularly those who are using their vast fortunes to achieve specific and ideologically driven ends are not evil or stupid, what are they exactly? We contend that Edreformers, whose perspective of the world is informed by neoliberal ideology, are just plain wrong about the problems and remedies related to public education in this country. Ultimately, the intentions of billionaires are irrelevant if the outcomes of their behaviors erode our democratic institutions. Education, as stated earlier, should be based on "participation, empowerment, and democracy" (Bennis, n.d., paragraph 1). However, when billionaires apply their wealth to circumvent democratic and participatory access to opportunities, with impunity, what happens to democracy in this country? We must, as a nation, be fully cognizant of the growing threat to our democracy. In his recently published text, Derek Blake (2020), a Constitutional scholar, noted, when discussing the current crisis with voting rights in the Unites States the relationship between public education and our democracy:

> While threats to the ballot are immediately understood as threats to democracy, attacks on public education are not always fully appreciated as such. But rest assured, just as the gift of public education has helped build up our democracy, taking it back threatens to tear down our democracy. (p. 16)

We are currently experiencing an open assault not only on our public institutions but also on our ability to participate as citizens in our democracy. We should carefully heed Blake's warnings and challenge even the most powerful and wealthiest among us to protect our democratic institutions.

While part of this chapter highlights how those with power and wealth choose to usurp the power of the public to advance their ideological agendas and gain further privilege, the overarching goal is to demonstrate how standardized testing, as part of the AIC, anchors most of the rhetorical and political arguments presented by Edreformers. Without the supposed objectivity of standardized testing data, whether that be NAEP results, state high-stakes exam data, SAT, ACT, etc., reformers would lack the simple, quantitative metrics, and all the symbolic and rhetorical power they carry, to persuade the general public to pursue educational choices that fail to be in their interests. And while not all choices proposed by Edreformers fail all students, as thus far demonstrated in this text, no amount of rhetoric will change how testing has marginalized and damaged our most vulnerable student populations. Additionally, our society has allowed those with unfathomable wealth to control our public institutions, in particular our public education system. They have consequently limited our capacity to engage in democratic and antiracist decision making and actions that could potentially benefit all students, teachers, and society as a whole. The AICs rhetorical capacity to instill fear in the populace has successfully limited our understanding of the dangers and threats the AIC poses to the future of public education. And while the rhetoric of fear undermines our democracy and potentially erodes our resolve to interrogate and challenge these threats, there is hope that various movements will undermine the goals of the AIC. As we will explore in the conclusion of the text, times are changing, awareness of inequity and injustice is building, and a door has been opened. The question is, will we have the courage as a society to walk through it?

References

Abundis, E. T., Crego-Emley, A., Baker, O., & Lema, J. (2017). Charter management organization report: Knowledge is power program. *Education Studies*. Retrieved from http://debsedstudies.org/knowledge-is-power-but-at-a-cost-kipp-cmo-report/.

Barkan, J. (2011, Winter). *Got dough? How billionaires rule our schools*. Retrieved from https://www.dissentmagazine.org/article/got-dough-how-billionaires-rule-our-schools.

Barshay, J. (2019, October 30). U.S. education achievement slides backwards: Substantial decrease in reading scores among the nation's eighth graders. *Covering Innovation & Inequality in Education*. Retrieved from https://hechingerreport.org/u-s-education-achievement-slides-backwards/.

Beder, S. (n.d.). Business-managed education. *Business-Managed Democracy*. Retrieved from https://www.herinst.org/BusinessManagedDemocracy/education/campaigns/Broad.html

Bennis, D. (n.d.). *What is democratic education?* Retrieved from Institute for Democratic Education in American website: http://democraticeducation.org/index.php/features/what-is-democratic-education/.

Berman Y., Ben-Jacob, E., & Shapira, Y. (2016). The dynamics of wealth inequality and the effect of income distribution. *PLoS One, 11*(4), e0154196. doi:10.1371/journal.pone.0154196.

Biddle, R. (2015, March 4). AFT's charter school hypocrisy. *Dropout Nation*. Retrieved from https://dropoutnation.net/2015/03/04/afts-charter-school-hypocrisy/.

Blake, D. (2020). *Schoolhouse burning: Public education and the assault on American democracy*. New York, NY: Hatchette Book Group.

Boser, U. (2012). *Race to the top: What have we learned from the states so far? A state-by-state evaluation of race to the top performance*. Washington, DC: Center for American Progress. Retrieved from https://files.eric.ed.gov/fulltext/ED535605.pdf.

Bowles S., & Gintis, H. (2011) *Schooling in capitalist America: Educational reform and the contradictions of economic life*. Chicago, IL: Haymarket Books.

Brandeis, J. (1932). New State Ice Co. v. Liebmann. *US Supreme Court, 285*.

Broadcenter. (n.d.-a) *Program profiles Marshall Tuck*. Retrieved from https://www.broadcenter.org/broad-residency/.

Broadcenter. (n.d.-b). *The broad residency in urban education*. Retrieved from https://www.broadcenter.org/broad-residency/.

Brooks, M. (1987). *Spaceballs [Film]*. Brooksfilms.

Brown, W. (2003). Neo-liberalism and the end of liberal democracy. *Theory & Event, 7*(1). doi:10.1353/tae.2003.0020.

Bryant, J. (2019, October 17). How billionaire charter school funders corrupted the school leadership pipeline. *Common Dreams*. Retrieved from https://www.commondreams.org/views/2019/10/17/%20how-billionaire-charter-school-funders-corrupted-school-leadership-pipeline#.

Center for Education Reform. (n.d.). *A nation still at risk? Results from the latest NAEP*. Washington, DC: Author. Retrieved from https://edreform.com/2019/10/naep2019/

Clough, C. (2015, September 15). Charters with Broad support show only a mixed return on investment. *LASchool Report*. Retrieved from http://laschoolreport.com/charters-with-broad-support-show-only-a-mixed-return-on-investment/.

Colorado Department of Education. (n.d.). *Teacher effectiveness office*. Colorado Department of Education. Retrieved from http://www.cde.state.co.us/educatoreffectiveness.

Common Core State Standards Initiative. (n.d.). *Frequently asked questions*. Retrieved from http://www.corestandards.org/about-the-standards/frequently-asked-questions/

CREDO. (n.d.). Retrieved from https://credo.stanford.edu/reports/%20MULTIPLE_CHOICE_CREDO.pdf.

Croft, S. J., Roberts, M. A., & Stenhouse, V. L. (2015). The perfect storm of education reform: High-stakes testing and teacher evaluation. *Social Justice, 42*(1). 70–92.

Dropout Nation. (n.d.). *About dropout nation.* Retrieved from https://dropoutnation.net/about/.

Ewing, E. L. (2018). *Ghosts in the schoolyard: Racism and school closings on Chicago's south side.* Chicago, IL: University of Chicago Press.

Fiorentini, R. (2014). Neoliberal policies, income distribution inequality and the financial Crisis. *Forum for Social Economics, 44*(2), 115–132.

Friedman, M. (1962). *Capitalism and freedom.* Chicago, IL: University of Chicago Press.

Friedman, F. (1970, September 13). The social responsibility of business is to increase its profits. *The New York Times.* Retrieved from https://www.nytimes.com/1970/09/13/archives/a-friedman-doctrine-the-social-responsibility-of-business-is-to.html.

Gangitano, A. (2019, June 13). Bill and Melinda Gates launch lobbying shop. *The Hill.* Retrieved from https://thehill.com/business-a-lobbying/448389- bill-and-melinda-launch-lobbying-shop.

Giroux, H. (2006). *America on the edge: Henry Giroux on politics, culture, and education.* New York, NY: Springer.

Hoffman, J. V., Assaf, L. C., & Paris, S. G. (2001). High-stakes testing in reading: Today in Texas, tomorrow? *The Reading Teacher, 54*(3), 482–492.

Hursh, D. (2007). Marketing education: The rise of standardized testing, accountability, competition, and markets in public education. In E. W. Ross & R. Gibson (Eds.), *Neoliberalism and education reform* (pp. 15–34). Cresskill, NJ: Hampton Press.

Kendi, I. X. (2016, October 20). Why the academic achievement gap is a racist idea. *Black Perspectives.* Retrieved from https://www.aaihs.org/why-the-academic-achievement-gap-is-a-racist-idea/.

Kendi, I. X. (2019). *How to be an antiracist.* New York, NY: Random House.

Kincheloe, J. L. (2001). Hope in the shadows: Restructuring debate over educational standards. In J. L. Kincheloe & D. K. Weil (Eds.), *Standards and schooling in the United States: An encyclopedia* (1st ed., Vol. 1, pp. 1–103). Santa Barbara, CA: ABC-CLIO.

Knoester, M., & Au, W. (2015). Standardized testing and school segregation: Like tinder for fire? *Race Ethnicity and Education, 20*(1), 1–14.

Knoester, M. & P. Parkison (2017). Seeing like a state: How education policy misreads what is important in schools. *Education Studies, 53*(3), 247–262.

Koretz, D. (2017). *The testing charade: Pretending to make schools better.* Chicago, IL:University of Chicago Press.

Leistyna, P. (2007). Corporate testing: Standards, profits, and the demise of the public sphere. *Teacher Education Quarterly, 34*(2), 59–84.

Lewis, A. (2018, March 7). Fulfilling the charter school promise: Accountability matters; So do freedom, fair funding, and strong operators. *The 74.* Retrieved from https://www.the74million.org/article/fulfilling-the-charter-school-promise-accountability-matters-so-does-freedom-fair-funding-and-strong-operators/.

Lipman, P. (2006). "No Child Left Behind": Globalization, privatization, and politics of inequality. In Ross & Gibson (Eds.), *Neoliberalism and Education Reform* (pp. 35–58). Cresskill, NJ:Hampton Press.

Mayeux, S., & Tani, K. (2016). Federalism anew. *American Journal of Legal History, 56*(1), 128–138.

Medvetz, T. (2012). *Think tanks in America*. Chicago, IL: The University of Chicago Press.

Metcalf, S. (2002, January 10). Reading between the lines: The new education law is a victory for Bush—and for his corporate allies. *The Nation*. Retrieved from https://www.thenation.com/article/archive/reading-between-lines/.

Milov, S. (2019). *The cigarette: A political history*. Cambridge, MA: Harvard University Press.

Moore, J., & Slater, W. (2011). *Bush's brain: how Karl Rove made George W. Bush presidential*. New York, NY: John Wiley & Sons.

Myers, T. (2018, October 21). Column: The $40-million race for California schools' chief is a proxy fight in a long-running war over education. *Los Angeles Times*. Retrieved from https://www.latimes.com/politics/la-pol-ca-road-map-thurmond-tuck-schools-charters-unions-20181021-story.html.

NAEP Report Card. (n.d.). *What to make of the 2019 results from the "Nation's Report Card"*. *Education Next*. Retrieved from https://www.educationnext.org/make-2019-results-nations-report-card.

National Commission on Excellence in Education. (1983). *A nation at risk: The imperative for educational reform*. Retrieved from https://edreform.com/wpcontent/uploads/2013/02/A_Nation_At_Risk_1983.pdf.

Oliff, P., & Leachman, M. (2011). New school year brings steep cuts in state funding for schools. *Center on Budget and Policy Priorities*, 7, 1–16.

Parkison, P. (2009). Political economy of NCLB: standards, testing and test scores. *The Educational Forum, 73*(1), 44–57.

Parkison, P. (2015). Catharsis in education: Rationalizing and reconciling. *Journal of Curriculum and Teaching Dialogue, 17*(2), 121–136.

Paufler, N. A. (2018). Declining morale, diminishing autonomy, and decreasing value: Principal reflections on a high-stakes teacher evaluation system. *International Journal of Education Policy and Leadership, 13*(8). 1–15.

Petrovic, J. E. (2019). *Unschooling critical pedagogy, unfixing schools*. New York, NY: Peter Lang.

Posner, R. (2006, December 31). Charitable foundations—Posner's comment. *The Becker-Posner Blog*. Retrieved from https://www.becker-posner-blog.com/2006/12/charitable-foundations—posners-comment.html.

PRWatch Editors. (2018, December 18). *Billionaire Eli Broad takes public education private*. Madison, WI: The Center for Media and Democracy. Retrieved from https://www.prwatch.org /news/2018/12/13434/billionaire-eli-broad-takes-public-education-private.

Ravitch, D. (2013). *Reign of error: The hoax of the privatization movement and the danger to America's public schools*. New York, NY: Vintage.

Ravitch, D. (2020). *Slaying Goliath: The passionate resistance to privatization and the fight to save America's public schools*. New York, NY: Knopf.

Reich, R. (2013, March 1). *What are foundations for? Boston Review*. Retrieved from http://bostonreview.net/forum/foundations-philanthropy-democracy.

Rodriguez, R. (2014, August 14). Bill Gates' market-driven experiments are not ready for prime-time public ed. *Teachers' Letters to Bill Gates*. Retrieved from https://teachersletterstobillgates.wordpress.com/.

Ross, W., & Gibson, R. (2007). *Neoliberalism and education reform*. New York, NY: Hampton Press.

Saltman, K. J. (2016). Corporate schooling meets corporate media: Standards, testing, and technophilia. *Review of Education Pedagogy and Cultural Studies, 38*(2), 105–123.

Schneider, M. K. (2015). *Common Core dilemma: Who owns our schools?* New York, NY: Teachers College Press.

Schneider, M. K. (2019, June 13). *About Gates' new, lobbying nonprofit: Don't kid yourself. Bill Gates already lobbies. Mercedes Schneider's Blog: Mostly education, with a smattering of politics and pinch of personal.* Retrieved from https://deutsch29.wordpress.com/2019/06/17/about-gates-new-lobbying-nonprofit-dont-%20kid-yourself-bill-gates-already-lobbies/

Strauss, V. (2014, June 9). How much Bill Gates's disappointing small-schools effort really cost? *Washington Post.* Retrieved from https://www.washingtonpost.com/news/answer-sheet/wp/2014/06/09/how-much-bill-gatess-disappointing-small-schools-effort-really-cost/.

Strauss, V. (2019, June 19). Bill and Melinda Gates have spent billions to drive their agenda on education and other issues. Now, they have created a lobbying group to push even more. *The Washington Post.* Retrieved from https://www.washingtonpost.com/education/2019/06/19/bill-melinda-gates-have-spent-billions-drive-their-agenda-education-other-issues-now-they-have-created-lobbying-group-push-even-more/.

Strong, R. W., Silver, H. F., & Perini, M. J. (2001). *Teaching what matters most: Standards and strategies for raising student achievement.* Alexandria, VA: Association for Supervision and Curriculum Development.

Thomas, P. L. (2012). Speaking empowerment to crisis: Unmasking accountability through critical discourse. In J. A. Gorlewski, B. J. Porfilio, & D. A. Gorlewski (Eds.). *Using standards and high-stakes testing for students: Exploiting power with critical pedagogy* (pp. 45–66). New York, NY: Peter Lang.

U.S. Const. amend. X.

U.S. Department of Education. (2014). *Race to the top phase 3 final results.* Retrieved from https://www2.ed.gov/programs/racetothetop/index.html.

U.S. Department of Education. (n.d.-a). *Elementary and Secondary Education Act of 1965.* Retrieved from https://www2.ed.gov/policy/elsec/leg/essa/legislation/index.html.

U.S. Department of Education. (n.d.-b). *Individuals with Disabilities Education Act (IDEA).* Retrieved from https://sites.ed.gov/idea/.

U.S. Department of Education. (n.d.-c). *Race to the top fund.* Retrieved from https://www2.ed.gov/programs/racetothetop/index.htm.

Walberg, H. J. (2010). *Advancing student achievement.* Stanford: Education Next Books/Hoover Institution Press, Stanford University.

West, C. (2017, January 9). Pity the sad legacy of Barack Obama. *The Guardian.* Retrieved from https://www.theguardian.com/commentisfree/2017/jan/09/barack-obama-legacy-presidency.

Yale School of Management. (2019, December 5). Yale SOM receives largest gift in its history from The Broad Foundation. *Yale News.* Retrieved from https://news.yale.edu/2019/12/05/yale-som-receives-largest-gift-its-history-broad-foundation[DC3].

Zhao, Y. (2018). *What works may hurt: Side effects in education.* New York, NY: Teachers College Press.

5

STUDENTS, TEACHERS, AND TESTING

An Existential Crisis in the Making

We have come to a time in history where it is difficult to justify the purpose of schooling. Under the social distancing realities of the recent global pandemic, school has taken on many forms, including Zoom sessions, online tests, and weekly packets. Even if and when school resumes to brick-and-mortar conditions, is it a good use of time and resources to send young people into large crowds where they will spend much of their time learning material, the main focus of which is to assess how students have "mastered" the standards? As Saltman (2017) points out, shouldn't we instead "emphasize knowledge and learning as the basis for collective forms of agency and self-governance, ethical life, and the creation of a sustainable future free of domination" (p. 3)? Saltman explains, "Policing the crisis also involves knowledge-making activities outside of schools" (p. 3). Is our current system the optimal approach to preparing future generations who will have to battle novel viruses, a degraded ecosystem, a crumbling infrastructure, and civil unrest, just to name some critical events?

Even for the most thoughtful, insightful, and optimistic among us, the daunting reality of our future prospects produces paralysis, for how do we contend with so many unknown possibilities when the primary goal of our neoliberal dominated culture, in reality, is to grow our economy and maintain the elite's dominance in the world. Saltman (2017) clearly articulates part of the existential crisis our society now faces: "Capitalist globalization results in a series of economic crises, worsening work opportunities and security. Transnational capitalists police the crisis, controlling and managing middle class, working class, and poor people" (p. 7). The neoliberal regime has successfully refocused our purpose from workers who produce to consumers who endlessly must consume to maintain economic growth and have relevance in society. Yet, research indicates that consumption, compared to experiences, for example, leads to less life satisfaction (Boujbel & d'Astous, 2012). This has additional devastating consequences to the human body and society as a whole, for to contend with the devastation wrought by the focus on consumption, we self-medicate and surrender control of our bodies to big pharma. We submit to the pharmaceutical industry's need to generate profit at all costs. One need only conduct a Google search of Purdue pharmaceuticals and the phrase "opioid addiction" to comprehend the sociopathic nature of these companies and their unquenching greed (Saltman, 2017). Thus, in this chapter, we focus our inquiry on students, teachers, and how the Assessment Industrial Complex (AIC) controls their bodies and minds and narrows the purpose of education to what can supposedly be measured and profited from. Specifically, we focus this next section on the impact testing has on students and continually revisit how intentions interact with other ecological elements, particularly curriculum, that are also tethered to the AIC.

Raison d'être of Schooling: Students as Test Takers

In tethering the curriculum to the AIC, it becomes convenient to think of curriculum as a given—rather than constructed—a predetermined list of skills, concepts, and facts that must be taught and eventually tested. This narrow understanding of curriculum reduces the students' role to primarily "test-taker." The student-test taker, a construct of the AIC ideology, also presents challenges to the development and implementation of curricula throughout educational institutions. Schools, programs, and curricula are marketed to test-takers and test administrators like any commodity for sale on the open market. Traditional curriculum planning questions are transformed in this new assessment- and accountability-driven context. Considerations of critical curriculum questions like the following become contingent on who has the power to decide these questions:

1. What is worth knowing?
2. What is worth learning?
3. What pedagogical approach has legitimacy? Why?

Rather than being focused upon contextual and axiological questions of content and pedagogy, curriculum development becomes a process of branding in the marketplace of test scores, differentiated instruction, and achievement gap reduction (Taubman, 2009).

We might ask what it is that makes being assessed so compelling, or in some sense what "forces" teachers to take assessments as ontologically necessary to education. The AIC, through test-based assessments, provides the scorekeeping mechanism through which individuals gauge their relative success or failure concerning other individuals. League tables and data walls present the scoreboard for all to see as the next round of student test-takers make their choice of school, program, and curriculum, as we demonstrated earlier through Koretz's (2017) account of red dots representing a student's value to the AIC. There are consequences for scorekeeping in schools as potential injustices derive from this system: economic maldistribution, exploitation, marginalization, deprivation, and cultural misrecognition and marginalization (Powers & Frandji, 2010). William Pinar (2012) expresses the consequences of this shift:

> Driven by such self-enclosed rituals, educational institutions devolve into cram schools, no longer about the world but, instead, about themselves, about those tests, apparently technical but altogether ideological, as students learn to process information without raising questions about that information or the process. What knowledge is of most worth? Is replaced with "what's your test score?" Such a shift in the curricular question ends critical thinking in the name of economic productivity. (p. 53)

To provide a context and a metric for the student test-taker, or their parent proxy, the government "…provides resources, enables local autonomy and responsibility for budgets, and at the same time offers performance guarantees" (Peters, 2011, p. 127). The student test-taker is empowered as an individual, and the common cultural conditions that once received consideration become degraded or narrowed into learning standards measured by standardized tests. This process of marketization also frames education as a positional good, a result of choice and effective exploitation of opportunities by a savvy consumer.

The AIC's Impact on Students: "It's Nobody's Fault But Their Own"

Expanding on Saltman's notion of the sociopathic tendencies of corporate America, we argue that students are victims of corporations' intentions and choices. Schools in general, and students specifically, are victims of corporations' willingness to exploit learners' self-doubt and need to compete to succeed. Students are forced to sit obediently to master content standards—standards that often are culturally and practically irrelevant to their lives; take an endless array of high-stakes standardized exams, often through the end of their high school years; and perform sufficiently on the SAT or ACT to have access and opportunity to attend college. As Saltman (2017) argues, "proper attention is demanded of students to display test-based performance outcomes that allow the student to compete for shrinking access to the world of work, income, and commodity consumption" (p. 20). Students who fail to comply with the rules and regulations of their school's expectations often end up on a different path. If that student is a male of color, that path can lead to underemployment, homelessness, prison, etc. (Alexander, 2012). Under these conditions, there is not much space for students to wrestle with the meaning of life or how they might improve upon their world. Instead, they are forced to comply with the assumption that educational policymakers and officials know what is best for them. The problem with this assumption is there is little evidence that people with power actually care about the needs and desires of future generations.

According to Giroux (2013), there is a "war on youth" (p. 88) aimed at instilling complacency to accept the status quo as an inevitable reality. Giroux (2013) posits this war is waged through an education deficit:

> The American public is suffering from an education deficit. By this I mean it exhibits a growing inability to think critically, question authority, be reflective, weigh evidence, discriminate between reasoned arguments and opinions, listen across differences, and engage the mutually informing relationship between private problems and broader public issues. This growing political and cultural illiteracy is not merely a problem of the individual, which points to simple ignorance. It is a collective and social problem that goes to the heart of the increasing attack on democratic public spheres and supportive public institutions that promote analytical capacities, thoughtful exchange, and a willingness to view knowledge as a resource of informed modes of individual and social agency. (pp. 29–30)

The AIC is at the crux of this deficit; it imposes intentional, structural, curricular, pedagogical, and evaluative limitations on what counts for education. The AIC provides the language and structures the narrative through which we have come to talk about education. The language we use is evidence of the AICs hegemony.

For example, Weiner (2014) demonstrates how standardized testing has impeded the imagination of young people to the point that they cannot think critically or creatively. Wiener describes an imaginary school, B.W. Gartenkrauter and the Critical School of Critical Thought and Imaginative Practice, where students actively participate in asking critical questions about their world and imagining ways to make it better. Although it may seem like wishful thinking, Weiner's imaginative school lays a realistic foundation for a world where students can explore questions like the following:

- What are we going to do about climate change?
- Why do people in Flint, Michigan, still have lead in their water?
- Why are our schools being resegregated?
- How many school shootings will it take to have sensible gun laws?
- Why are we at war with Iraq?
- Who will pay for today's wars?
- Who will pay for the tax cuts and subsidies to billionaires and corporations?
- Why do so many people of color experience police brutality?

Rather than explore these questions, students today learn that the answers have already been determined by the adults (Gottlieb, 2015), and if they want to get ahead in life, they better do well on the tests. No pair of tests exemplifies this better than the SAT and ACT, the premier college admissions and, thus, high-stakes exams required, until recently, by most four-year universities and colleges.

The AIC's Cost to Education: Grit and Perseverance

We continue to explore some of the underpinning theoretical problems of treating students as test-takers later in the chapter. However, first, it is important to recognize how education funding and resources are siphoned away from students and their schools to the benefit of the AIC. Likewise, when students lack funding and resources to be successful, they are blamed for deficits produced that are, in actuality, generated by the AIC and the neoliberal rhetoric that enables it.

As mentioned in previous chapters, the AIC costs a great deal. From a monetary perspective, a Brookings Institute study found standardized testing costs states $1.7 billion per year (Chingos, 2012). It is difficult to justify spending such an excessive amount of money allocated to testing on one hand while, on the other hand, imposing austerity measures on schools. These measures have forced schools to cut services like school nurses and counseling as well as reduce funding for non-tested programs like physical education, art, and music (Giroux, 2013; Ravitch, 2015). For students, this austerity is often communicated as an opportunity to build their sense of perseverance or what Duckworth (2016), Tough (2012), and others refer to as "grit." Grit is based on the notion that individuals can achieve academic and professional success by overcoming obstacles and challenges—often over a long period. Although Duckworth (2016) argues that grit does not correlate with higher test scores, she suggests that grit is a matter of individuals making individual decisions. As individuals deny their immediate desires and needs in favor of long-term goals, they become grittier. Under the rhetoric of grit, a lack of educational access and resources can help individual students fortify their grit. This framework makes it difficult to address systemic educational inequalities because the onus of educational success is placed on individual students and teachers. According to Saltman (2014), "grit reinforces a description of educational processes that underlie consumer culture, that is, a feeling of scarcity in which the student is constantly denied the fulfillment of desires and needs, through nobody's fault but their own" (p. 53):

Goodman (2018) also takes a critical perspective on the notion of grit. Recently he argued that grit, "growth mindset" (Dweck, 2015), and other terms intended to help motivate individual student success in school are problematic because they do not account for systemic realities. Goodman offers a definitive, albeit not exhaustive, list of some of the conditions students face, which neither grit, nor perseverance, nor any other personal attribute can necessarily overcome:

> Defining students and their relative grittiness as the problem that needs fixing fails to address the banking and real estate markets that segregate their families in unsafe and unhealthy housing, or the child welfare and justice systems that serve to break up the families of low-income students of color and incarcerate, detain and deport their parents…Improving students' disposition to learning won't change these conditions. (p. 3)

The AIC leaves little to no room for the curriculum to help students understand and address these conditions. So, rather than question the system, students are taught that their perceived shortcomings are ultimately their fault. This rhetoric enables the AIC to amass power and profits while states impose austerity measures on vulnerable schools. Saltman (2014) concludes,

> Austerity education is not only about a turn to repressive control of youth in favor of amassing profits for the rich, creating a docile and disciplined workforce as the conditions of work and life are worsened for the majority of citizens. It is also about the rightist project of capturing public space such as schools to actively produce politically illiterate, socially uncritical, and un-self critical subject positions for youth to occupy. It involves a project of teaching teachers and students to understand learning and rationality through submission to authority, and miseducating them to comprehend their alienation as a failure of individual gumption rather than as a constitutive part of development informed by a social formation and economy that depends upon the making of alienation. (p. 55)

Under the rhetoric of this system, students are ultimately responsible for their success. If students just have enough "grit" and "growth mindset," they too can live the American dream. And, when they don't, "It's nobody's fault but their own" (except for maybe teachers).

The School-to-Prison Pipeline: Repeated Trope or Material Reality?

In 2010, the Advancement Project released a report entitled *Test, Punish, and Push Out: How "Zero-Tolerance" and High-Stakes Testing Funnel Youth into the School-to-Prison Pipeline* (2010). The report, broken down into four major sections, examines the relationship between high-stakes testing and the school-to-prison pipeline. Beginning with a history of the movement to address the war on crime, the authors discuss the origins of zero-tolerance policies and later, its relationship to high stakes testing. They provide a clarion call of the dangers posed by this relationship:

> The educational opportunities of millions of children across this country are continuously put at risk by zero tolerance school discipline and high-stakes testing. This new brand of punitive educational policy has brought students of all races, in all 50 states perilously close to being high school dropouts and/or entering the juvenile and criminal justice systems. (p. 7)

Further, as the report underscores, the outcomes of the relationship between zero-tolerance policies in schools and the high-stakes testing mandates most severely impacts "students of color and low-income students, who, too often, are being punished for losing a race in which their peers were given a head start" (p. 7). The report provides detailed arguments for how zero-tolerance policies and high-stakes standardized tests work in tandem to push students out of school. For example, because high-stakes testing drives (i.e., anchors) educational decision making, teachers and administrators enforce policies permitting the punishment and/or removal of misbehaving students from the classroom. This practice, the thinking goes, prevents "bad kids" from affecting the learning of "good ones." Further noted, the message communicated to educators from high-stakes testing policies is that the "focus should not be on nurturing and educating each child to reach their full potential; their focus should be on getting as many students as possible to reach the level of 'proficiency'" (p. 28).

The report also states that there seems to be a direct correlation between "the consequences attached to test results and the severity of school disciplinary practices, meaning districts that face the most test pressure will be the most inclined toward punitive measures" (p. 28). By combining the focus on testing with the need to minimize classroom disruptions, schools place teachers in the difficult position of having to choose between their self-interests and that of their students, even if this means focusing classroom instructional time on test preparation and narrowing their approach to curriculum. Ultimately, one must question if this really is a choice at all; if their students do not perform proficiently on high-stakes exams following their district and state's expectations, there are consequences for teachers, administrators, and their students. Nevertheless, there is much collateral damage from such choices. Students' boredom is a significant consequence of excessive test preparation, something that occurs disproportionately in schools with a majority-minority population of students.

Additionally, when schools face the prospect of consequences for low test scores, they become more likely to enact more punitive policies. These policies include increased suspensions, expulsions, grade retention, and school-based arrests. And these outcomes, too, excessively affect students of color and those in poverty. According to the Advancement Project Report (Community Partners, 2010),

> One thing has remained constant: students of color disproportionately bear the burden of harsh school discipline. There are two key components to that inequity: unequal treatment at the individual level, and unequal use of zero tolerance at the systemic level. (p. 15)

More disturbing is that disruptions are all too often classified as "illegal offenses" that criminalize typical childhood behaviors for which school resource officers are on hand to address:

> Having police nearby transforms the daily school experience into a minefield of potential crimes: fighting in the hallway becomes a "battery"

> or even "aggravated battery;" swiping a classmate's headphones can be classified as "theft" or "robbery;" and talking back to a teacher or officer is "disorderly conduct." (p. 16)

This conditional reality shifts the incentive structure for teachers from providing a nurturing, caring curriculum and instructional practices that serve the interests of their students, to emphasizing test preparation and removing students from classrooms and schools that disturb that focus. "[Z]ero tolerance becomes a tool used to address the inevitable backlash from the daily grind of filling in test-booklet bubbles and being subjected to a narrowed, lackluster curriculum" (p. 28). The student is to blame rather than an inequitable and racist system that disengages students via futile classroom experiences.

The Advancement Project Report (Community Partners, 2010) underscores how these inequalities perpetuate the school-to-prison pipeline and maintain institutional racism. Sadly, the synthesis of zero- tolerance policies, coupled with a heavy emphasis on high-stakes testing preparation, shapes and determines the teacher–student relationship in damaging and long-lasting ways, further upending the school ecology stasis. Students, in particular students of color, struggle to see themselves as stakeholders in their education and vital members of the communities in which they live. The AIC, and proponents of criminalizing typical student behavior, reinforces a neoliberal ideology, one that places economics (i.e., testing equates to profit as does the prison system) and political expediency (i.e., we will not tolerate disruptive students) above the needs of our youth, particularly those who have the greatest needs.

How the AIC Shapes Teachers and Their Students

The impact of the AIC on teachers has been both cumulative and relentless. From being burdened with excessive responsibilities both in and out of school contexts, to being scapegoats for many of society's failures, teachers have struggled to maintain a modicum of professionalism and purpose in their work. It is difficult to identify a specific point in time when teachers became part of the "problem" within the discourse of education, but what is certain is that the data from testing is consistently used to reinforce the failures of teachers and schools. Because schools and teachers know they will be evaluated by their students' test scores, raising test scores becomes the goal of teaching and learning. Psychologist and social scientist Donald Campbell (1979) studied how people change their behavior when they know they are being evaluated. He found that these changes in behavior can distort evaluation processes and produce unintended adverse effects. Campbell's findings eventually became known as "Campbell's Law."

Koretz (2017) recently detailed how Campbell's law can cause teachers and, in fact, entire school systems to teach directly to the test and even cheat to raise test scores. There are numerous examples of Campbell's Law as an outcome of testing pressures in schools—including what the Georgia Bureau of Investigation found to be widespread cheating among teachers, principals, and administrators in the Atlanta Public School system (Aronson, Murphy, & Saultz, 2016). Relating this concept to the school ecology, we argue that high-stakes testing can influence teacher intentions and distort the very purpose of school. When test scores become the source of sustenance for a system (student, teacher, school), then the system adapts to live on that material. Test scores, within the school ecology, is the food that is consumed, the air that is breathed. Likewise, because so much is at stake with standardized assessments, students and parents are also susceptible to focusing their intentions on testing. These pressures and distorted intentions can even lead to cheating (Rothstein, 2008). For example, we recently saw a well-documented example of how far parents will go to safeguard their children's future and the privileges associated with their wealth and status. In 2019, the news broke of a college admissions bribery scandal—also known as "Operation Varsity Blues"—where at least 53 individuals (including celebrities like Lori Loughlin, Mossimo Giannulli, and Felicity Huffman) were charged with several crimes: fraudulently inflating SAT and ACT scores, bribing college officials, and other unethical acts, all to secure their children's acceptance into prestigious universities (Hextrum, 2019). As previously discussed, these types of high-stakes standardized exams have numerous negative impacts on students, teachers, parents and society. While we cannot directly blame the tests for parents' choices to use their privilege and wealth to cheat the college admissions processes, the system, as Campbell's Law demonstrates, creates a toxic environment of desperation and abuse.

Although it is not technically cheating, another outcome of the AIC is the wide use of what Saltman (2017) refers to as "smart drugs." According to Saltman,

> ADHD, which has seen massive recent increases in diagnosis since 2000, is defined as a difficulty in paying attention, restlessness, and hyperactivity. By 2010, nearly one in three US children ages 2–17 had been diagnosed as suffering ADHD, and by 2012 the diagnosis of ADHD had risen 66% in the prior decade. Ballooning rates of diagnosis have been met with unprecedented prescriptions, principally for the amphetamine pharmaceutical drugs Adderall and Ritalin. (p. 19)

As Saltman demonstrates, the rise in the use of "smart drugs" follows along the same timeline as the rise of standardized tests and are later used to advantage students on high-stakes college exams—such as the SAT and ACT. Amphetamines function as a type of technology, a technology that helps control students' thoughts and bodies so they can concentrate in school and perform well on tests.

Although they are certainly different types of technology, the AIC has forced a variety of technologies upon teachers and students, and some of these technologies are not developmentally appropriate for children. Conn (2014) saw first-hand how rural elementary teachers defied their sensibilities and understandings of their students' developmental needs to expose them to technologies, such as typing skills, that were believed to be necessary to show "growth" on standardized assessments. A veteran third-grade teacher admitted, "I worry that we are too focused on growth and achievement... not always thinking about their [students'] developmental needs" (Conn, 2014, p. 138). Similarly, Alfie Kohn (2004) observed how children's developmental needs are sacrificed for testing:

> Every few days, there is fresh evidence of how teaching is being narrowed and dumbed down, standardized and scripted—with poor and minority students getting the worst of the deal as usual. I have an overstuffed file of evidence detailing what we're sacrificing on the altar of accountability, from developmentally appropriate education for little children to rich, project-based learning for older ones, from music to field trips to class discussions. (p. 20)

From an intentional perspective, attending to the AIC has certainly overshadowed what we know to be good for child development. Armstrong (2006) likens the imposition of the standards movement on child development to sweatshops of the industrial revolution:

> We've returned to the "hard times" of Charles Dickens [Mr. Gradgrind in *Hard Times* (1854) by Charles Dickens]: that is to say, we've transformed too many of our classrooms into content skills and factories reminiscent of the sweatshops of the industrial revolution instead of making them into exciting places for birthing wonderful ideas. (p. 89)

Though Armstrong's critique may seem harsh, it is clear that AIC has yielded a public education system in which standards and standardized tests matter more than the developmental needs of students. Eisner (2001) too points out that "Education has evolved from a form of human development serving personal and civic need into a product our nation produces to compete in a global economy" (p. 370). Conversely, in 1968 Finland began intentionally considering developmental processes in education, and this attention to developmental conditions has contributed to Finland's rise in international acclaim concerning education (Aho, Pitkanen, & Sahlberg, 2006; Sahlberg, 2007). In 2009, Finland's Ministry of Education explained how human development fits into their national goals for education (as cited by Darling-Hammond, 2010):

> The aim (of Finnish education policy) is a coherent policy geared to educational equity and a high level of education among the population as a

whole. The principle of lifelong learning entails that everyone has lifelong learning skills and opportunities to develop their knowledge and skills in different learning environments throughout their lifespan. (p. 163)

Finland's educational model is based on a system where "highly trained teachers design the curriculum around very lean national standards" (p. 167) with high regard to the developmental needs of students. Developmental considerations include child-centered schedule structures, intentional cooperative learning activities, less focus on rote memory skills, greater focus on critical thinking skills, narrative feedback from teachers addressing descriptions of students' learning process, and no external standardized tests used to rank students (Aho et al., 2006; Darling-Hammond, 2010; Sahlberg, 2007). Adequate funding and strong partnerships also have helped Finland's success in education (Darling-Hammond, 2010), but the Finnish educational model pays attention to human development.

In addition to Finland's educational success, both South Korea and Singapore experienced distinguished educational success in the international arena, and they, too, have focused on human development as a major feature in their educational reform efforts (Darling-Hammond, 2010). In the case of Finland, raising PISA scores were not utilized as the motivation to move schools in a more phenomenon-driven direction. The students' and society's happiness, as measured by the OECD's "Better Life Index" was pointed to as a critical outcome of school changes (Zhao, 2018). While countries around the world recognize the importance of making educational decisions around child development, public schools and classrooms are anchored to testing-based decisions from the AIC.

Similar to our discussion in Chapter 2 about "Good Intentions and the Road to Hell," good intentions can still lead to bad outcomes. Under the influence of the AIC, the American education system has wrought an upside-down world where well-intended teachers, parents, and students base their decisions on what will be tested—as opposed to creating conditions for lifelong learning and human development. While it is important to demonstrate how testing can influence parent and student intentions as well, in the next section, we focus on how testing shifts teachers' intentions and undermines their professionalism by limiting their agency in relation to the curriculum and their students' learning.

Under a neoliberal perspective of education, following a line of curiosity, wherever it may lead, would be an act of educational heresy at worst and a waste of time at best. Curiosity is for hobbies, not education. For Edreformers, the focus of education must remain on the representation of the value of one's "learning experiences." Often, this translates to a diploma, certificate, test score, or some other marketable symbol of knowledge acquisition. The shift toward a concern for preparation for employment and the role of credentialing in the sorting and hiring processes that graduates will face as they enter the job market is striking. Kindergarten is the beginning of college and career readiness. Discussions of development, intellectual curiosity, generative experience, and transformational learning may be present, but it is submerged under the rhetoric of career readiness and accountability. Having experienced this same transition in the realm of teacher preparation, where alternative certification and teacher preparation pathways control the dialogue, teacher candidates seek the path of least resistance into the teaching profession and then find themselves ill-equipped to sustain themselves in the classroom (Parkison, 2016).

Like the Common Core Standards, CAEP reduces the preparation (a reductionist term in and of itself) of teachers to a specified set of predetermined outcomes aligned to college and career readiness standards. The entire body of CAEP standards can and has been reduced, for the sake of efficiency we imagine, to one page that includes five standards and a set of sub-standards. Yet, the extensive body of literature, both empirical and theoretical, attests to the vast amount of depth and breadth afforded the teaching profession. For us teacher educators, there are many issues with the CAEP standards, and that discussion is beyond the purview of this chapter. But one major affront concerning CAEP regarding the preparation of preservice and in-service teachers is the lack of care about equity and justice. Yet, in the CAEP handbook (which includes 71 pages of standards, substandards, rubrics, etc.) the term *assessment* is mentioned over 70 times, *equity* is mentioned a whopping four times, and nowhere in the entire body of CAEP standards is the phrase *Social Justice* included. As Schwarz (2016) points out, "Equity is reflected in the number of times CAEP repeats *ALL* students, and learning about student differences is included, but "social justice" is not mentioned" (p. 44). Faithfully following a neoliberal doctrine toward education, CAEP and other bodies of standards (e.g., INTASC, NCTM, NCTE, etc.) are reductionist and prescriptive. And also, faithful to the AIC ideology, to ensure that approved programs adhere to the standards, CAEP forces accredited programs to assess, assess, and assess some more through standardized tests of professional knowledge and content-area knowledge.

The standardization, focus on testing and credentialing of teachers, and students in general, affect how individuals conceive of themselves and their capabilities. On the one hand, they augment the power of the individual in relation to the world: increased access and availability have brought education to a larger segment of the population and increased individual productivity. This shift has made it possible for more people to graduate from high school, achieve associate's and bachelor's degrees, and for states and communities to lay claim to the signifiers of educational achievement. On the other hand, they have diminished the significance of particular individuals within the world: with the use of standardization and credentialing, workers have become effectively indistinguishable, interchangeable, not unlike the products they will make. In this climate, the same credential that is used to sell young people the need for education has become valueless. Further, the same credentialing devalues the student upon completion of their degree. Access to the credential has been expanded to the point at which it is no longer useful as a tool to differentiate.

This lack of utility applies to teachers as well. As many advocates of charter schools attest, teachers are more similar than different in terms of their role in and value to schools; if teachers are dissatisfied with the conditions of their employment, they are free to leave and easy enough to replace (Parkison, 2016). Given alternative certification routes, finding a "certified teacher" to replace an experienced and knowledgeable one is perceived as not that difficult, and not even necessary. Hence, teachers are perceived as generic rather than unique and of professional value. Further, one study found that "the odds of a charter school teacher leaving the profession versus staying in the same school were 130% greater than those of a traditional public school teacher" (Stuit & Smith, 2010, p. 2). In this context, teachers no longer see themselves as professionals with agency; rather, they understand that they are dispensable and that "anyone" who is "willing and able" can teach. Further, Kirylo and Aldridge (2019) point out that

> today, with the shortage of teachers coupled with an acute need for qualified teachers to be placed in highly-challenging settings, the need has justified a focus on the quantity, which has particularly enabled the point of view that teaching is a trade that simply requires training. (p. 42)

None of this bodes well for teachers, students, or society. Preparing to teach in a way that meets *all* students' needs requires more than demonstrating proficiency on a series of benchmarks, competencies, assessments, and certification exams that are contrived and controlled by external accrediting agencies and profitable testing companies. This way of envisioning education also narrows the curriculum through the prism of standardization, assessment, and credentialing; thus, we lose what is unique and essential about the potential of curriculum to ground teaching and learning in what makes us human.

The AIC: Enframing the School Ecology

As entire school ecologies are tethered to testing, every attempt at teaching/ learning/ translation within the AIC enframed system is itself already assessed at a higher/prior administrative or policy level. This is an assumed necessary condition for teaching and learning to be possible. Assessment through the systems developed by the AIC makes the student performances within teaching events data points that can be tracked, aggregated, analyzed, and posted (again, consider Koretz's examples shared earlier). Assessment as data points turns a learning trace into oppressive symbolic violence—equating students and teachers to the data they generate. Assessment as data hides complexity by covering over or rendering invisible supposed unnecessary details—individual life experiences and the lived ecology of the students, school, and community are pushed to the margin and out of the conversation about education. Eisner (2001) relates this to issues of equity stating

> Educational equity is much more than just allowing students to cross the threshold of the school. It has to do with what students find after they do so... But when we narrow the program so that there is only a limited array of areas in which assessment occurs and performance is honored, youngsters whose aptitudes and interests lie elsewhere are going to be marginalized. (p. 372)

Within the AIC-dominated education narrative, literacy, math, and, sometimes, science are given priority. Students interested in the humanities, fine arts, and most trades find themselves situated as secondary stakeholders having little input in the decisions that most impact them. The measures that truly impact are related to college readiness, not necessarily career readiness. No matter a student's interests or aptitudes, aspirations or goals, the system incentivizes courses and curricula that will impact test scores, producing the data-trace needed to document success and failure. This homogeneity is crucial to the continued influence of the AIC and the education system it promotes and sustains through assessment.

The assessment produces a remarkable continuity which suggests at least a sufficient level of sameness to endure from one lesson to the next—this is exactly what makes curriculum work within the AIC regime, what enables classrooms to run, processes and procedures to persist, and so forth. Curriculum maps are developed to sequence lessons to maximize "coverage" of academic standards—especially the power standards that are predicted to be represented most frequently on the high-stakes tests. Pacing guides are generated to ensure control over the implementation of the curriculum maps, a forced accountability for teachers, and a burden for administrators. Assessments of all kinds are the anchor for demonstrating fidelity to the system of accountability. Each lesson is linked to a map derived from the standards. Each lesson is evaluated as valuable or not based on the alignment of the learning objectives to the standards. The reason for being of each lesson is its link to the standards and its potential to move test scores in a positive direction. When the date from the tests indicate a gap in a particular standard domain, the lessons from that domain are scrutinized. In order to be timely in the identification of these gaps, schools have implemented increasing levels of standardized formative assessments. Indeed, this is precisely what gives assessment its power as "data" and symbolic value. Its power to translate teaching and learning is only secured in its ongoing enactment as data sources, in other words, in its assumed or taken for granted ontological necessity for validation (Biesta, 2009; Parkison, 2015). Thus, once established, there is remarkable incentive to maintain assessments as the data sources and symbolic values they have become, that is, power and control over educational outcomes. But this is not secure; it is always possible to be otherwise.

Enframing Students and Teachers

All assessments are fundamentally performative. By performative we mean that in its ongoing enactment assessment produces what it assumes. Assessment achieves its performativity through its assumed necessity as the data source needed for the evaluation of instruction and learning. Clearly, some degree of repetition (or sameness) is the constitutive condition for the translation of teaching and learning to endure, from one lesson to another. Linking or sequencing lessons so that students develop a level of predictive anticipation of what comes next and what is expected of them is part of education, part of the formation of learning habits. However, iterative repetition also immediately constrains—that is to say, it becomes the necessary condition for that which is repeated to be exactly a repetition (Foucault, 1970; Nietzsche, 1982). Repetition is the foundation of habits. Like most habits, learning, or the demonstration of the learning through performance on assessments, relies upon repetition. Thus, the extension of teaching and learning is only legitimated within the schooling system if instruction conforms to the assessment that will be taken as part of the lesson as a repetition.

Learning is the performative outcome of assessed material enactments; they are essentially intra-relational. There is always a multiplicity of assessed teachings and learnings entangled in the enactment of any particular lesson. What gets repeated and habituated involves the data points that are recorded, analyzed, and traced as part of the accountability system. Although there are always infinite possibilities for the future of education and schooling to be otherwise, it is nevertheless, in a certain and important sense, remarkably the same. This is exactly due to the performative power of assessment as a repetition of the generation of linked data points that are then displayed on data walls and school league tables. In their ongoing enactment, these multiplicities of entangled assessed lessons intra-act or self-validate and provide mutual legitimation. Once a specific enactment, or form of enactment, is legitimated, all other enactments of teaching and learning are marginalized. This enactment is a form of symbolic violence as the instrument of the AICs consolidation of power and oppression of education.

Every assessment is already within, and already encapsulates, other lessons which are taken as necessary for its becoming. Thus, in its recursive performativity, assessment always already enframes: "Enframing is the gathering together that belongs to that setting upon which sets upon man, i.e., challenges him forth, to reveal the real, in the mode of ordering, as standing reserve" (Heidegger, 1977, p. 20). We would suggest that the enframing of assessment does not only translate and reveal the world as "standing reserve" (which might be the performative outcome particular to modern schooling, if one applies Heidegger's analysis of technology). Instead, it more generally reveals schools, teachers, and students as always already assessed—enframed within assessment.

As data points become the symbolic representation of students and schools, the continued assessment of students and schools is necessarily essential to education with the AIC-dominated paradigm. As Heidegger suggests, every epoch has its dominant frame, the frame that orders and encapsulates other ways of becoming, and thereby translates and performatively constitutes the becoming of beings as being essentially this or that sort of becoming. Therefore, we assert that as schools, classrooms, teachers, and students implicitly or explicitly take up and draw on lessons and procedures/processes which assessment renders possible, those same lessons and procedures/processes also performatively constitute them (and reveal the world to them) as already assessment, in a particular manner of being. As extended beings, teachers and students are always already enframed by assessment.

Discussion of the Testing Industry and Extension of Agency

Within the schooling system that has emerged since *A Nation at Risk,* it can be claimed that the transition from a primary curriculum-driven educational system to an assessment-driven educational system happened over a period of time with a variety of intermediate stages of standardization and accountability. Prior to No Child Left Behind, the development and use of assessment driven lessons or scripts were mostly limited to a group of teachers and students framed as "at-risk" or "under-served" (Apple, 2006). Labels, operationalization strategies, and data systems were used to legitimate a symbolically violent and oppressive system. This framing was code for racial, gender, and socioeconomic biases within policy and institutional education.

We also note that the major reason for the development of these assessment-driven lessons was to facilitate neoliberal competition/scorekeeping and for administrative accountability, especially connected with increased globalization and urbanization: in other words, to extend/enact agency at a distance in situations where agency needed to reach beyond the local community and where accuracy in repetition was determined to be most important—in matters of power and wealth. As Taubman (2009) asserts, "all measure derives from the center of power" (p. 112). Those who have power control the meaning and implications of the measurement. In the case of the AIC, this power has been used to marginalize Black and Brown students in ways that perpetuate inequity and injustice. Moreover, racism is embodied in the AIC, forged in its core principles and values.

As discussed in the introduction, it is interesting to note that education advocates like Horace Mann utilized early assessments to professionalize teaching and standardized learning. As William Reese (2013) writes:

> Mann had praised written tests in official reports and in editorials in the *Common School Journal.* Such tests were sometimes used to screen prospective teachers in Europe and some American cities and to vet pupils for the nations' fledgling high schools. After additional reading and conversations with educators during their travels, Mann and Howe recognized broader uses for written examinations. By yielding *numerical* scores, tests could help measure both teacher proficiency and pupil achievement, allowing comparisons within and between schools. (p. 59)

By idiosyncratically adopting assessment strategies from the German context without regard for their function or cultural context in Germany, Mann and Howe began the process of turning assessments into symbols of some abstract ideal. They did not relate these assessments to the context within which they would play a role—thus allowing a basic form of testing to emerge outside the elite circles of the honors degree aspirants. As mentioned above, assessment is often a bricolage of what is available at the moment (i.e., it is essentially unfounded).

Utilizing material assessment of the curriculum, the political governance of the schooling system, centered on local interests and needs, can be replaced with more general policies centered on standards and global competitiveness (Beadie, 2004; Biesta, 2014; Parkison, 2015). From this assessment translation, a new and radically different form of schooling becomes possible if not required—what we refer to as a symbolically violent system of assessment and accountability. The discourse of standards, assessment, and accountability permeates contemporary educational debate to the extent that alternative discourses such as creativity, risk, intellectual engagement, and the notion of being an educated person are silenced, or at best marginalized. Eisner (2002) expands on the negative impact of focusing on assessment, "the message that we send to students is that what really matters in their education are their test scores" (p. 369). But to his additional point, this undermines the purpose of educating a student: "Students are, it can be said, rationally planning their education. But such planning has very little to do with intellectual life, where risk taking, exploration, uncertainty, and speculation are what it's about" (p. 369). In Biesta's (2009) terms, the language of learnification has usurped the educational endeavor. Agendas such as school improvement plans, achievement targets, and behavioral intervention programs are deeply rooted in the way of looking at the world that resonates with Heidegger's notion of technological enframing (Heidegger, 1977).

The enframing imposed upon the educational system by the AIC is so pervasive that it has become largely invisible as a taken-for-granted way of seeing the schooling endeavor. Indeed, it is this invisibility that gives it its power in shaping teaching and learning, and that results in those engaged in the educative endeavor becoming increasingly estranged. As Heidegger (1977) explains,

> But we are delivered over to it in the worst possible way when we regard it as something neutral; for this conception of it, to which today we particularly like to do homage, makes us utterly blind to the essence of technology. (p. 4)

Commentators have argued that the enframing manifests itself in virtually all areas of schooling, from the governance of childhood through the school improvement agenda, to teacher education and educational research. We do not argue that agendas such as school improvement, intervention, or evidence-based practice have no value; however, we do argue that they are currently located within an invisible technological and dehumanizing neoliberal agenda.

An important term Heidegger introduces is *Bestand*, or loosely translated "standing reserve" (Heidegger, 1977). As standing reserve, individuals are re-legated to a potential pool of energy to be called on as and when needed. Teachers and students are thus rendered as part of *Bestand*, important primarily because of their potential in the immediate goal of improving performance and the longer-term goal of enhancing economic competitiveness. Interaction and dialectic between standardized tests and test scores produce a distinct economy of exchange. The relationships created within the symbolic exchange of standardized tests get consumed in the violence of test scores as they are utilized within accountability systems at the state, district, school, teacher and student level representing a significant aspect of the AIC regime.

Although the AIC asserts the noble objective of equity of educational opportunity, the reality of differentiation and stratification is hard to ignore (Apple, 2006). Test scores become signifiers of status and are linked to the allocation of resources within the system (Craig, 2004). As these test scores become fetishes of status and privilege, the connection to academic standards and the standardized tests themselves gets lost (Beadie, 2004; Parkison, 2009; Siegel, 2004). As test scores are transfigured into symbols of status and privilege—both curriculum and relationships of teaching and learning become submerged within the system. Baudrillard (1981) demonstrates the significance of this transition:

> There is no articulation between these three forms (which describe general political economy) and symbolic exchange. There is only symbolic "exchange," which defines itself precisely as something distinct from, and beyond value and code. All forms of value (object, commodity or sign) must be negated in order to inaugurate symbolic exchange. This is the radical rupture of the field of value. (p. 125)

Not only does the AIC rupture the field of value, but it also ruptures the purpose of school. For example, Uhrmacher (2005) detail the influence of school/classroom-community relationships on ecological systems within schools. However, as Conn (2016) found, assessment can over-power those relationships and dominate school/classroom ecologies. In this case, Colorado's *Educator Effectiveness Law* (2010) tethered teacher evaluation to the AIC, and this relationship forced teachers to focus their curriculum and instruction on what would be tested, even when they disagreed with the tests. Teachers and students have little choice but to base their educational decisions on what will be tested.

What Does It All Add Up To? The Cost of the AIC

As we conclude this chapter, consider Eisner's ecology of school improvement (1988). The AIC restricts the school's ecological interactions from occurring across intentional, structural, curricular, pedagogical, and evaluative dimensions; thus, unless something changes, those who function within the school ecology will only know a world anchored within the realm of the AIC. There is security in the anchor. But we must ask ourselves, "Is this really what we want?" Is this truly the purpose of education, and who decides (Tenam-Zemach & Flynn, 2011)?

The AIC was constructed, at least in part, to improve educational circumstances; have educational circumstances improved? We think not. Instead, we find what Darling-Hammond (2006) rhetorically asks, "How might the goal of improving schools actually, paradoxically, undermine them?" (p. 661) We find an education system that spends hundreds of billions annually on testing and yet cannot afford school nurses and counselors (Kohn, 2000; Pak, 2016). We find plenty of time and resources for tested subjects at the cost of non-tested subjects and parts of school (like art, music, physical education, civics, and recess). We find scripted curricula and pacing guides that sacrifice teacher and student autonomy. We find demoralized teachers and teacher shortages (Nicols & Berliner, 2008). We find students in the United States will take an average of 112 standardized tests throughout their K–12 career (Hart et al., 2015). We find the AIC costs time away from learning (Jones, Jones, & Hargrove, 2007). We find the AIC compounds problems of inequality by taking resources away from the most vulnerable of students (Clotfelter, Ladd, Vigdor, & Diaz, 2004; Conn, 2015). We find a system that is increasingly segregated along racial and socioeconomic lines (Knoester & Au, 2017). The AIC costs our society its democracy. Eisner asks, "What does it all add up to" (2002, p. 233)? It adds up to us being able to afford the cost of the AIC.

References

Advancement Project Report (Community Partners). (2010). *Test, punish, and push out: How "zero tolerance" and high-stakes testing funnel youth into the school-to-prison pipeline.* Retrieved from https://b.3cdn.net/advancement/d05cb2181a4545db07_r2im6caqe.pdf.

Aho, E., Pitkanen, K., & Sahlberg, P. (2006). *Policy development and reform principles of basic and secondary education in Finland since 1968. Education working paper series (2).* Washington, DC: Human Development Network Education.

Alexander, M. (2012). *The new Jim crow: Mass incarceration in the age of colorblindness.* New York, NY: The New Press.

Apple, M. (2006). *Educating the "right" way: Markets, standards, God, and inequality* (2nd ed.). London, UK: Routledge.

Armstrong, T. (2006). *The best schools: How human development research should inform educational practice.* Alexandria, VA: Association for Supervision and Curriculum Development.

Aronson, B., Murphy, K. M., & Saultz, A. (2016). Under pressure in Atlanta: School accountability and special education practices during the cheating scandal. *Teachers College Record, 118*(14), n14.

Baudrillard, J. (1981). *For a critique of the political economy of the sign.* St. Louis, MO: Telo Press.

Beadie, N. (2004). Moral errors and strategic mistakes: Lessons from the history of student accountability. In K. Sirotnik (Ed.), *Holding accountability accountable: What ought to matter in public education.* New York, NY: Teachers College Press.

Biesta, G. J. (2009). Good education in an age of measurement: On the need to reconnect with the question of purpose in education. *Educational Assessment, Evaluation and Accountability, 21,* 33–46. 10.1007/s11092-008-9064-9

Biesta, G. J. (2014). *The beautiful risk of education.* New York, NY: Paradigm Publishers.

Boujbel, L., & d'Astous, A. (2012). Voluntary simplicity and life satisfaction: Exploring the mediating role of consumption desires. *Journal of Consumer Behaviour, 11*(6), 487–494.

Campbell, D. T. (1979). Assessing the impact of planned social change. *Evaluation and Program Planning, 2*(1), 67–90. 10.1016/0149-7189(79)90048-X

Chingos, M. M. (2012, November 29). *Strength in numbers: State spending on K-12 assessment systems.* Washington, DC: Brookings Institution. Retrieved from https://www.brookings.edu/research/strength-in-numbers-state-spending-on-k-12-assessment-systems/.

Clotfelter, C. T., Ladd, H. F., Vigdor, J. L., & Diaz, R. A. (2004). Do school accountability systems make it more difficult for low-performing schools to attract and retain high-quality teachers? *Journal of Policy Analysis and Management, 23*(2), 251–271.

Council for the Accreditation of Educator Preparation. (2019). Standard 1: Content and pedagogical knowledge. Retrieved from http://caepnet.org/standards/standard-1.

Cochran-Smith, M., Feiman-Nemser, S., McIntyre, D. J., & Demers, K. E. (Eds.). (2008). *Handbook of research on teacher education: Enduring questions in changing contexts.* London, UK: Routledge.

Conn, D. R. (2014). *Attending to growth: Implications of the Colorado Growth Model for three rural schools (Doctoral dissertation).* Greeley, CO: University of Northern Colorado, Ebsco.

Conn, D. R. (2015). Juxtaposition: The coexistence of traditional Navajo and standards based curricula. *The Qualitative Report, 20*(5), 618–635.

Conn, D. R. (2016). What are we doing to kids here? *Curriculum and Teaching Dialogue, 18*(1-2), 25–40.

Craig, C. (2004). The dragon in school backyards: The influence of mandated testing on school context and educators' narrative knowing. *Teachers College Press, 106*(6), 1229–1257.

Darling-Hammond, L. (2006). No Child Left Behind and high school reform. *Harvard Educational Review, 76*(4), 642–667.

Darling-Hammond, L. (2010). *The flat world and education: How America's commitment to equity will determine our future.* New York, NY: Teacher's College Press.

Duckworth, A. (2016). *Grit: The power of passion and perseverance* (Vol. 234). New York, NY: Scribner.

Dweck, C. (2015, September 22). *Carol Dweck revisits the 'growth mindset.' Education Week.* Retrieved from https://www.edweek.org/ew/articles/2015/09/23/carol-dweck-revisits-the-growth-mindset.html.

Eisner, E. W. (2001). What does it mean to say a school is doing well? *Phi Delta Kappan, 82*(5), 367–372.

Eisner, E. W. (2002). *The educational imagination: On the design and evaluation of educational programs* (4th ed.). New York, NY: Macmillan.

Fantilli, R. D., & McDougall, D. (2009). A study of novice teachers: Challenges and supports in the first years. *Teaching and Teacher Education, 25*(6), 814–825.

Foucault, M. (1970). *The order of things: An archaeology of the human sciences* (L. M. choses Trans.). New York, NY: Vintage Books.

Giroux, H. A. (2013). *America's education deficit and the war on youth: Reform beyond electoral politics.* New York, NY: NYU Press.

Goodman, S. (2018). *It's not about grit: Trauma, inequity, and the power of transformative teaching.* New York, NY: Teachers College Press.

Gottlieb, D. (2015). *Education reform and the concept of good teaching.* London, UK: Routledge.

Greenblatt, D. (2018). Neoliberalism and teacher certification. *Policy Futures in Education, 16*(6), 804–827.

Hart, R., Casserly M., Uzzell, R., Palacios M., Corcoran A., & Spurgeon, L. (2015, October). *Student testing in America's great city schools: An inventory and preliminary analysis.* Retrieved from Council of the Great City Schools' website: https://www.cgcs. org/cms/lib/DC00001581/Centricity/Domain/87/Testing%20Report.pdf.

Heidegger, M. (1977). *The question concerning technology and other essays* (W. Lovitt Trans.). New York, NY: Harper Torchbooks.

Hextrum, K. (2019). Operation varsity blues: Disguising the legal capital exchanges and white property interests in athletic admissions. *Higher Education Politics & Economics, 5*(1), 15–32.

Jones, G. M., Jones, B. D., & Hargrove, T. (2007). *The unintended consequences of high-stakes testing.* Lanham, MD: Rowman & Littlefield.

Kirylo, J. D., & Aldridge, J. (2019). *A turning point in teacher education: A time for resistance, reflection and change.* Lanham, MD: Rowman & Littlefield.

Knoester, M., & Au, W. (2017). Standardized testing and school segregation: Like tinder for fire? *Race Ethnicity and Education, 20*(1), 1–14.

Kohn, A. (2000). *Standardized testing and its victims.* Retrieved from http://www.alfiekohn. org/article/standardized-testing-victims/.

Kohn, A. (2004). Test today, privatize tomorrow. *The Education Digest, 70*(1), 14–22.

Koretz, D. (2017). *The testing charade: Pretending to make schools better.* Chicago, IL: University of Chicago Press.

Kumashiro, K. K. (2012). *Bad teacher! How blaming teachers distorts the bigger picture.* New York, NY: Teachers College Press.

Nicols, S., & Berliner, D. (2008). Testing the joy out of learning, educational leadership. *Educational Leadership, 65*(6), 14–18.

Nietzsche, F. (1982). Twilight of the idols. In F. Nietzsche, & W. Kaufmann (Ed.), *The Portable Nietzsche* (pp. 463–563). New York, NY: Penguin Books.

Pak, K. (2016, June 22). *The high costs of high-stakes.* Retrieved from The Center on Standards, Alignment, Instruction and Learning website: www.c-sail.org/resources/ blog/high-costs-high-stakes-testing.

Parkison, P. (2009). Political economy of NCLB: Standards, testing and test scores. *The Educational Forum, 73*(1), 44–57.

Parkison, P. (2015). Catharsis in education: Rationalizing and reconciling. *Curriculum and Teaching Dialogue, 17*(2), 121–135.

Parkison, P. (2016). Teacher as commodity: Controlling the supply chain. *The Educational Forum, 80*(1), 107–123.

Peter, M. A. (2011). *Neoliberalism and after?: Education, social policy, and the crisis of Western capitalism*. New York: Peter Lang.

Pinar, W. (2012). *What is curriculum theory?* (2 nd ed.). New York, NY: Routledge.

Power, S., & Frandji, D. (2010). Education markets, the new politics of recognition and the increasing fatalism towards inequality. *Journal of Education Policy, 25*(3), 385–396.

Ravitch, D. (2015). *The death and life of the great American school system: How testing and choice are undermining education*. New York, NY: Basic Books.

Reese, W. J. (2013). *Testing wars in the public schools: A forgotten history*. Cambridge, MA: Harvard University Press.

Rothstein, R. (2008, June). The corruption of school accountability: How experience with quantitative measurements in other sectors can inform the use of high-stakes test scores in education. *The School Administrator, 65*(6), 14–18.

Sahlberg, P. (2007). Education policies for raising student learning: The Finnish approach. *Journal of Education Policy, 22*(2), 147–171.

Saltman, K. J. (2014). Neoliberalism and corporate school reform: "Failure" and "creative destruction". *Review of Education, Pedagogy, and Cultural Studies, 36*(4), 249–259.

Saltman, K. J. (2017). *Scripted bodies: Corporate power, smart technologies, and the undoing of public education*. London, UK: Routledge.

Schwarz, G. (2016). CAEP and the decline of curriculum and teaching in an age of techne. *Curriculum and Teaching Dialogue, 18*(1–2), 41–54.

Sessions, D. (2020, January 14). How college became a commodity: Market-based thinking is at the heart of how academe thinks of itself. That's a travesty. *The Chronicle Review*. Retrieved from https://www.chronicle.com/interactives/how-college-became-a-commodity

Siegel, H. (2004). What out to matter in public schooling: Judgment, standards, and responsible accountability. In K. Sirotnik (Ed.), *Holding accountability accountable: What out to matter in public education*. New York, NY: Teachers College Press.

Stuit, D., & Smith, T. M. (2010, August). *Teacher turnover in charter schools (Research Brief)*. Retrieved from https://www.researchgate.net/publication/255600494_.

Taubman, P. M. (2009). *Teaching by numbers: Deconstructing the discourse of standards and accountability in education*. London, UK: Routledge.

Tenam-Zemach, M., & Flynn, J. (2011). America's race to the top, our fall from grace. *Curriculum & Teaching Dialogue, 13*(1/2), 113–124.

Tough, P. (2012). *How children succeed: Grit, curiosity, and the hidden power of character*. Boston, MA: Houghton Mifflin Harcourt.

Uhrmacher, P. B. (2005). *Building his palette of scholarship: A biographical sketch of Elliot Eisner. Intricate palette: Working the ideas of Elliot Eisner*. Upper Saddle River, NJ: Prentice Hall.

Weiner, E. J. (2014). *Deschooling the imagination: Critical thought as social practice*. London, UK: Routledge.

Zhao, Y. (2018). *What works may hurt: Side effects in education*. New York, NY: Teachers College Press.

6

A PATH TO HOPE AND CHANGE

The Time is Now

In Chapter 6, A Path to Hope and Change: The Time is Now, we explore current anti-testing movements and demonstrate how they are disrupting the AIC. We discuss the CoVid-19 pandemic and exemplify some impacts it is having on high-stakes, standardized testing. The pandemic has opened a door providing us the opportunity to walk through it and dismantle the AIC. But the door will un-doubtedly close if our society does nothing. Hence, we call for actions, ones that will hopefully lead to the abolishment of the Assessment Industrial Complex.

In this concluding chapter, we revisit the overarching arguments presented in this book and offer a change of perspective, one informed by optimism and hope for a better future for our children and society. In the end, no matter the material benefits of standardized, high-stakes testing, it is primarily about money, power, and control of knowledge. We have yet to see unbiased, empirical data that supports the position that standardized testing has helped any teacher or child in any meaningful, holistic way. Furthermore, as we have consistently demonstrated throughout this book, there are significant issues with the implementation of standardized tests and the utilization of its data. It has not only failed to benefit our most vulnerable students, but it has also done detrimental harm to many of them, and other students, their schools, and communities. There are too many points of contention and cracks in the foundation to justify the Assessment Industrial Complex (AIC). The current COVID-19 crisis has provided a clear and demonstrable amplification of the cracks in the testing façade. We also have hope that change is occurring due to certain movements offering a different narrative, narratives grounded in equity, social justice, and a shared belief that testing and the AIC fail to keep their promises. This chapter explores some of these fissures and movements, providing a path forward that potentially can ameliorate current inequities and injustices for the betterment of students, teachers, and society as a whole.

COVID -19 and the Future of the AIC

Throughout the process of writing this book, we felt confident in unraveling the AIC and exposing how it operates. Still, we did not foresee the coming of a global pandemic and the civil unrest in response to ongoing racial inequalities and police brutality. These two historic events have disrupted the AIC and the indefinite reliance on standardized tests to make educational decisions. Because of COVID -19 and the social distancing guidelines set by the Center for Disease Control and Prevention, for the first time in 18 years, the U.S. Department of Education did not require states to administer standardized assessments. Despite attempts by the College Board and school districts across the country to require AP exams to be taken online in students' homes, it quickly became apparent that these efforts were unsuccessful. In fact, the National Center for Fair & Open Testing (FairTest) filed a class-action lawsuit against Educational Testing Services (ETS), the College Entrance Examination Board, and the College Board because of the well-documented technical problems associated with requiring students' to take the AP Exam from home (Jaschik, 2020).

One outcome of resistance to the AIC, and its intersection with the pandemic, is the tsunami of colleges and universities choosing to drop the requirement for an ACT or SAT score for at least a year (National Association for College Admission Counseling; NACAC, 2020). The mammoth organizations that own the tests, ACT Inc. and the College Board, are struggling in the new environment, more so since the California University system will no longer accept the SAT or ACT in its admissions processes (Hubler, 2020). In fact, a recent report released by the National Association for College Admission Counseling (NACAC) explores the admissions issues confronting colleges and universities regarding standardized testing policies during and beyond COVID -19. In the section on Assessing Student Potential, the report states,

> As originally envisioned, college admission exams were intended to provide a "common yardstick" as the population of students expanded. Moreover, early in their history, college admission exams held the promise of finding the "diamond in the rough," or high-performing students in settings where colleges traditionally had not sought them. However, time has changed much about the founding purposes and assumptions behind these exams. Indeed, the very notions of "diamonds in the rough" and even the "common yardstick" are culturally suspect—are not all students capable of success given equal opportunity? (p. 10)

Additionally, the report acknowledges how the SAT and ACT are "deeply embedded" (NACAC, 2020, p. 1) in the enrollment processes and functions of colleges and universities across the United States and the world. The report describes how the use of standardized testing scores can "range from searching for prospective students to guiding the selection process, allocating financial aid and scholarship funds, and forecasting yield and retention. Student test scores are even used by third parties to rate our institutional quality and our creditworthiness" (p. 1). Because the task force insisted they utilize a lens focused on "access and equity" (p. 2) throughout their approach to their work, they focused on several essential guiding questions, the first being: "what are the ways in which college admission exams contribute to or detract from post-secondary access and success for a diverse set of students" (p. 2)? Resolving that standardized testing perpetuates inequity and diminished access for students to the undergraduate admissions process, the task force was determined to offer a "the most stringent of reviews" (p. 2) before offering specific recommendations to American institutions of higher education. Ultimately, the task force recommends six "key considerations" that colleges and universities follow throughout their decision-making admissions processes:

> Consider the public good.
> Be student-centered.
> Focus on students' success.
> Be transparent and clearly stated.
> Include a plan for conducting frequent reviews.
> Consider unintended consequences. (p. 3)

The report concludes by emphasizing that standardized tests are only one component of many in the college admissions process that leads to inequitable college admissions practices. Further, as professionals who participate in the college admissions counseling process, the task force insists that colleges must address what they can control and change: "standardized testing is one area that the task force believes institutions … should feel empowered to reexamine and to demand that, regardless of location and circumstance, such tests foster equity and access for their applicants" (NACAC, 2020, p. 19). Moreover, according to the report, COVID -19 provides the opportunity for constructing meaningful change in how colleges across the nation approach and utilize admissions tests like the SAT and ACT, and for reconsidering the role of equity throughout the entire college admissions process.

Upon reading this report, we as parents, educators, and social justice advocates interpreted its recommendations with optimism and hope. While the report does not suggest that colleges and universities abandon standardized testing for college admissions applications in the future, it clearly states that institutions of higher education have acknowledged the disruptions caused by COVID-19. They acknowledge the "threat to fairness, equity, and access posed by maintaining testing requirements" (NACAC, 2020, p. 6) during the pandemic. Additionally, the task force mentions the test-optional movement pointing out that COVID-19 has accelerated it. We now have hope that post-secondary institutions will use this pandemic as an opportunity to revisit their mission to offer equitable access to all students wishing to attend college and consider how standardized admissions exams limit such access and opportunity. As the report states, "institutions must commit to showing evidence to the public that they are making good on this renewed commitment to students that higher education can be an engine of opportunity and social mobility for all" (pp. 8–9). Though the conditions and realities of COVID-19 have given some reprieve from the AIC, we must be mindful of the fact that the AIC will look for opportunities to reinstate itself as the anchor of all things education. COVID-19 certainly exposed and undermined the AIC, but without systemic changes, we should expect it to come roaring back with a vengeance to make up for lost revenue in 2020. Thus, as the AIC is now vulnerable, it is imperative that we use these critical moments in history to expose further and finally abolish the AIC.

Anti-testing Movements: Disrupting the AIC

While COVID -19 kept students from taking tests, the murder of George Floyd by several Minneapolis Police Officers ignited a significant global response to ongoing police brutality and systemic inequalities. At the beginning of our time writing this book, not very many people we talked to knew the term antiracism; today, Ibram X Kendi's *How to Be an Antiracist* (2019)—which we reference and discuss throughout this book—is a best-selling book in the United States. *Antiracist* has become a common term that large numbers of people are beginning to understand and discuss openly for the first time. People from all walks of life are examining systemic inequalities and White supremacy. As Strauss (2020) put it,

> Protesters in the streets are looking for justice not only in policing and the courts. They also want social, economic and educational justice. Though educators have long known that students need more than tests to thrive and that schools must address more than academics, there is a new awareness among the people who make policy.
>
> *(paragraph 30)*

Furthermore, a series of cheating scandals—including the Varsity Blues Cheating Scandal (Strauss, 2020)—have exposed how wealth and privilege can inflate standardized test scores and game the system. Like the *Wizard of Oz*, the curtain has been pulled back. The shock of the number of changes that have proliferated over the first half of this decade is nearly incomprehensible. However, this door of opportunity will not stay open indefinitely. We must, as a society, use the current unrest and clarity of the moment to demand educational justice for our students.

Antiracism Movement and the Impact on the AIC

Part of deconstructing the AIC is by approaching all education decision making with an antiracist lens. To reiterate, Kendi (2019) argues that one is either racist or antiracist, and to be antiracist means, among other things, to ensure that the "laws, rules, procedures, processes, regulations, and guidelines that govern people" (p. 18) respect the autonomy, needs, and rights of every individual who will be impacted by them. Whether one agrees with Kendi's binary approach to defining racism (Colman, 2019) or not, to effect change that will positively alter the lives of students, teachers, etc., we must reconceive how we understand the experiences of students of color and poverty in the system of education. Moreover, we must address the relationship of standardized testing to policies, practices, and procedures that continue to oppress and marginalize entire student populations. A part of several social justice and other movements acknowledges and contends with the role of standardized testing and the importance of framing their approach as antiracist. Thus, we chose to underscore several of the significant and current movements and the actions they are taking to subvert the AIC.

Although recent events have disrupted the AIC, The National Center for Fair and Open Testing—also known as "FairTest"—has been disrupting standardized testing since 1985 (National Center for Fair & Open Testing, n.d.). Created by civil rights leaders' groups, FairTest exposes how standardized assessments can be detrimental to academic achievement and equal opportunity. Their work includes campaigns against the AIC and advocating for alternatives to standardized assessments. Education columnist Valerie Strauss (2014) credits FairTest's influence on the anti-testing movement:

> Across the nation, resistance to test overuse and misuse reached unprecedented heights in the spring of 2014. The rapidly growing movement built on significant test opposition unleashed in 2013. This year, resistance erupted in more states with far more participants, and it won notable victories, such as ending, lessening or postponing graduation exams in at least eight states and easing or ending grade promotion tests.
>
> *(paragraph 2)*

This momentum has since intensified, and it is bipartisan. George Will (2014), Logan Albright (2017), Jim Geraghty (2020), and other conservative political pundits have become critical of standardized assessments. We suspect conservative opposition to high-stakes testing is based on partisan opposition to the Obama Presidency. FreedomWorks, the Cato Institute, Americans for Prosperity, and the Koch Brothers have all launched campaigns to undermine the adoption and implementation of the Common Core Standards to stoke populist fear and anger at the Obama Administration (Williams, 2014); evidently, opposition from the Right continues. At the core of contemporary conservative critiques to high-stakes testing is a legitimate concern for the collateral damage and obvious limitations of the AIC. Geraghty (2020) provides an example of non-partisan critique from a conservative lens:

But a lot of young people—and probably a lot of their parents—live in fear that they will be judged by tests that measure their value and potential on seemingly arbitrary criteria, and that if they screw up on that, they'll be shunted off into some category of "lesser" people. There's a reason this pops up so much in everything from young adult fiction to dystopian films. Teenagers in particular feel like their parents don't understand them, their teachers don't understand them, their community doesn't understand them ... so how the heck is a giant multiple-choice test going to understand what their talents are and what they're capable of?

(paragraph 8)

It is becoming clear to many conservatives that the AIC threatens their ideals of freedom, liberty, and self-determination.

As you can recall from Chapters 2 and 3, the liberal support for the AIC initially hinged on the assumption that standardized testing would improve the learning conditions for all students—particularly students of color. This assumption makes it difficult to challenge the AIC because there is real trepidation that students will not receive the funding and support they need for public education without standardized testing (NACAC, 2020). Before the passage of the Every Student Succeeds Act (ESSA), 12 prominent American civil rights groups—including the National Association for the Advancement of Colored People (NAACP), Urban League, and the National Council of La Raza—doubled down on their support for standardized assessment by issuing in a joint statement admonishing the opt-out movement:

Standardized tests, as "high stakes tests," have been misused over time to deny opportunity and undermine the educational purpose of schools, actions we have never supported and will never condone. But the anti-testing efforts that appear to be growing in states across the nation, like in Colorado and New York, would sabotage important data and rob us of the right to know how our students are faring. When parents "opt out" of tests—even when out of protest for legitimate concerns—they're not only making a choice for their own child, they're inadvertently making a choice to undermine efforts to improve schools for every child.

(Leadership Conference on Civil and Human Rights, 2015, paragraph 4)

However, their position has changed since issuing this statement. The NAACP now opposes standardized testing (Vasquez, Brewer, & Ojeda, 2018), and there are a growing number of people within the civil rights movement turning. In his essay, "Why Opting Out is good for Students of Color," Hagopian (2016) argues:

Our task must be to build multiracial alliances in the opt out movement that can produce the kind of solidarity it will take to defeat a testing juggernaut that is particularly destructive to communities of color—while causing great damage to all of our schools. And while we must begin by standing up to the multibillion dollar testing industry by opting out, we must also create a vision for an uprising that opts *in* to antiracist curriculum, ethnic studies programs, wrap around services to support the academic and social and emotional development of students, programs to recruit teachers of color, restorative justice programs that eliminate zero tolerance discipline practices, and beyond.

(paragraph 21)

Additionally, campaigns like "Let Us Teach!"—led by Chicago Teachers Union president Karen Lewis—affect change and opposition to the AIC at the grassroots level. Communities of color and low-income are opting out of testing at nearly the same rate as Whiter and wealthier communities (Uetricht, 2014). It's like the old saying, "Scratch a lie; find a thief." As those seeking equity and social justice continue to scratch the lies of neoliberalism and White supremacy, they will find the AIC.

Black Lives Matter

While the Black Lives Matter (BLM) movement is not specifically an "anti-testing movement," no statement better encapsulates the relationship between the BLM movement, systemic racism, and standardized testing than the following one from the Schott Foundation for Public Education:

> If we acknowledge the truth about the systemic racism in our country, we must also acknowledge the impact that racism has on our children and their classrooms. For us, #BlackLivesMatter is more than just a hashtag or social media post. #BlackLivesMatter is a policy doctrine that should govern how we think about safety, health care, the economy and certainly our nation's public schools.

(Perry et al., 2020, paragraph 2)

The BLM movement began "as a chapter-based, member-led organization whose mission was to build local power and to intervene when violence was inflicted on Black communities by the state and vigilantes" (Black Lives Matter, 2020, paragraph 1). However, the movement is now more broadly "committed to struggling together and to imagining and creating a world free of anti-Blackness, where every Black person has the social, economic, and political power to thrive" (paragraph 2). In fact, and as already demonstrated, education is now listed as a focus for BLM's #WhatMatters2020 Invest-Divest campaign. More specifically BML is seeking,

> A constitutional right at the state and federal level to a fully-funded education which includes a clear articulation of the right to: a free education for all,

special protections for queer and trans students, wrap-around services, social workers, free health services (including reproductive body autonomy), a curriculum that acknowledges and addresses students' material and cultural needs, physical activity and recreation, high-quality food, free daycare, and freedom from unwarranted search, seizure or arrest. (p. 1)

The AIC stands in opposition to these aims. Not only does the AIC impose curriculum while ignoring students' material and cultural needs, but it also disproportionately limits students of color from attending selective colleges. A study from Carnevale and Strohl (2013) found that over 80% of White new post-secondary students go to 468 of the most selective colleges. In contrast, 72% of LatinX and 68% of African-American new post-secondary students go to two-year open-access schools. Soares (2020) builds on these findings to conclude:

One highly significant factor that contributes to the racial stratification of higher education in general, and to the decline in black students at very selective colleges in particular, is the growing weight of race in determining SAT/ACT scores. For too long and by too many, these test scores have been taken as a proxy for individual intellectual merit, when they have always correlated more highly with demographics than with academic performance. Over the last decade, race has become a higher predictor of SAT/ACT test scores than parent education or family income.

(paragraph 5)

The effects of the BLM have extended to and influenced other organizations, including post-secondary institutions. According to the Associated Press (Skretta, 2020, July 16), in response to the BLM movement and other social justice initiatives, a new committee on racial reconciliation was formed by the National Association of Basketball Coaches. In a joint statement, the committee co-chairs Frank Martin (South Carolina University) and Tommy Amaker (Harvard University) said standardized tests "no longer have a place in intercollegiate athletics or education at large," and that eliminating them would be "an important step towards combating educational inequality" (paragraph 3). It is not just coaches who are rethinking standardized testing. Before the pandemic, in 2019, nearly 50 institutions announced that they would adopt a test-optional policy (NACAC, 2020). Since the pandemic began, three-fifths of Four-Year Colleges and Universities are going "test-optional" for their admission requirements by Fall 2021 (Fair Testing, 2020).

Thus, there is hope that change is imminent; it is time for institutions of higher education to reassess the purpose of education and their role in influencing the drivers of K–12 education. The test-optional, test-flexible, and test-blind options (NACAC, 2020) alone will not address the myriad of inequities that exist in higher education admissions and other educational processes. We need an honest, deliberate, and transparent debate about the impact of standardized testing on all levels and aspects of education and the lives of all students. One conclusion will come from such a debate: It is time to abolish the AIC.

It Is Time to Pull the Weeds: Abolishing the AIC

The everyday life of the classroom, free of thematic framing and concealment, becomes the horizon for the emergence of individual identity and whole communities. To ask how we are doing in educating our next generation is to reclaim the personal view of learning as critically involved with others in the development and definition of ourselves. Overcoming assessment, as currently enframed, would reinvigorate the relationships between teacher–student and student–student as a reclaiming of the ecology of education. By asking how we are doing, we are advocating for increased dialogue and dynamism in education, and working against the passive, compliant reliance on quantitative, mechanical methods of assessment and instruction as prescribed by the AIC hegemony. Let us begin the process of reframing education and schooling by thinking differently about assessment. Let us engage with all stakeholders to determine what forms of data we need to collect and then collectively analyze the data in ways that facilitate social justice and equity throughout our education system. These actions will lead us to shift the ground upon which we think assessment from the repetition of the same (homogeneous) to the process of generating and valuing differences through deterritorialized responses (Deleuze & Guattari, 1987; Hroch, 2014).

Accepting the critical task of education—facilitating an enduring interest in the world—is to think differently about students, to see them as people in the process of becoming. Thinking differently requires us to move beyond (outside of) education's current assessment focus on accumulation and exchange of information in which what is learned effectively sustains the habituated circulation of knowledge and the maintenance of the status quo. Thinking about students as people in the process of becoming means valuing learning as a process of transformation, the process of coming to think differently, and becoming other in the process. Accepting the critical and transformative task of education requires supporting thinking differently from the fetishized learning norms and facilitating the production of a diverse range of critical, creative, and generative ideas that promote students' desiring and experiencing of joy in expressing their emerging capacities.

Whether you lean progressive or conservative, we must take action to abolish the AIC. We must call out the AIC for what it is—a eugenist, racist, classist construct that has been used to perpetuate White supremacy and other forms of inequality. We recognize that some will argue that we cannot remove the AIC without something to put in its place to ensure students are getting the funding and support they need. We have heard it said, "if you are going to pull weeds, you must plant flowers in their place." However, in this case, the weeds are literally based on eugenics, White Supremacy, and an absurd, neoliberal presumption (or what some may simply call a lie) that the testing industry is going to fix deep systemic inequalities. These weeds are diverting billions of dollars from public schools, and they are destroying our public education system.

There certainly are "flowers" we can plant to make sense of whether a school is doing well, and if students are getting the support they need. We are intrigued by Eisner's (2002) model of evaluation and more holistic ways of evaluating educational circumstances; however, these "flowers" must be antiracist at their core. And, first thing's first: It's time to pull the weeds. It's time to cut the rope from the anchor. The time is now to abolish the AIC. Whether we protest, opt our children out of testing, or contact our elected representatives, we must take action—particularly considering our moment in history. We have a binary choice, and inaction only further enables the lies, exploitation, anxiety, theft, symbolic violence, racism, and White supremacy perpetuated by the AIC. Now is our moment in history to do the right thing. Now is the moment to abolish the AIC.

References

Albright, L. (2017, February 11). 5 smart reasons to abolish the Department of Education. *Conservative Review.* Retrieved from https://www.conservativereview.com/news/5-smart-reasons-to-abolish-the-department-of-education/.

Black Lives Matter (2020). A vision for Black lives: Policy demands for Black power, freedom, & justice . Education Amendment Brief. https://m4bl.org/policy-platforms/invest-divest/.

Carnevale A. P., & Strohl, J. (2013, July). *Separate and unequal: How higher education reinforces the intergenerational reproduction of white racial privilege.* Washington, DC: Georgetown University. Retrieved from https://cew.georgetown.edu/wp-content/uploads/SeparateUnequal.FR_.pdf.

Colman, H. (2019, October 27). How to be an anti-intellectual: A lauded book about antiracism is wrong on its facts and in its assumptions. *City Journal.* Retrieved from https://www.city-journal.org/how-to-be-an-antiracist.

Deleuze, G., & Guattari, F. (1987). *A thousand plateaus: Capitalism and schizophrenia.* (B. Massumi Trans.). London, UK: Athlone Press.

Eisner, E. W. (2002). *The educational imagination: On the design and evaluation of educational programs* (4th ed.). New York, NY: Macmillan.

Geraghty, J. (2020, February 6). Standardized testing and populism. *National Review.* Retrieved from https://www.nationalreview.com/corner/standardized-testing-and-populism/.

Hagopian, J. (2016, March 9). *Six reasons why the opt out movement is good for students and parents of color. The Progressive.* Retrieved from https://progressive.org/public-school-shakedown/six-reasons-opt-movement-good-students-parents-color/.

Hroch, P. (2014). Deleuze, Guattari, and environmental pedagogy and politics. In M. Carlin & J. Wallin (Eds.), *Deleuze and Guattari, politics and education* (pp. 49–75). London, UK: Bloomsbury.

Hubler, S. (2020, May 24). University of California will end use of SAT and ACT in admissions. *The New York Times.* Retrieved from https://www.nytimes.com/2020/05/21/us/university-california-sat-act.html.

Jaschik, S. (2020, May, 21). College board sued over AP exams. *Inside Higher Ed.* Retrieved from https://www.insidehighered.com/quicktakes/2020/05/21/college-board-sued-over-ap-exams.

Kendi, I. X. (2019). *How to be an antiracist.* Random House.

The Leadership Conference on Civil & Human Rights (2015). *Civil rights groups: "We oppose anti-testing efforts." The Leadership Conference on Civil & Human Rights.* https://civilrights.org/2015/05/05/civil-rights-groups-we-oppose-anti-testing-efforts/.

National Association for College Admission Counseling (NACAC). (2020). *Access to higher education: The role of standardized Testing in the time of COVID-19 And beyond Guidance for colleges.* Retrieved from https://www.nacacnet.org/globalassets/documents/knowledge-center/nacac_testingtaskforcereport.pdf.

National Center for Fair & Open Testing (FairTest). (n.d.). Retrieved from https://www.fairtest.org/.

Perry, A., Brown, J., Blair, k., Fowler, R., Gates, S. D., & Loftin, T. D. (2020, July, 21). *9 things to make Black lives matter in our public schools.* New York, NY: Schott Foundation for Public Education. Retrieved from http://schottfoundation.org/blog/2020/07/21/9-things-make-black-lives-matter-our-public-schools.

Skretta, D. (2020). College hoops coaches move to eliminate standardized testing. APNews. Retrieved from: https://apnews.com/article/43d638e5f32b848595f3b02d570bd87a.

Singer, S. (2018, July 18). The NAACP once again opposes high stakes standardized testing! Gadfly On The Wall Blog, Retrieved from: https://gadflyonthewallblog.com/2018/07/18/the-naacp-once-again-opposes-high-stakes-standardized-testing/.

Soares, J. A. (2020, June 25). *Dismantling white supremacy includes ending racist tests like the SAT and ACT.* New York, NY: Teachers College Press. Retrieved from https://www.tcpress.com/blog/dismantling-white-supremacy-includes-racist-tests-sat-act/.

Strauss, V. (2014, October 30). The rise of the anti-standardized testing movement. *The Washington Post.* Retrieved from https://www.washingtonpost.com/news/answer-sheet/wp/2014/10/30/the-rise-of-the-anti-standardized-testing-movement.

Strauss, V. (2020, February 15). There's a lot of talk about changing college admissions after the Varsity Blues scandal—don't hold your breath. *The Washington Post.* Retrieved from https://www.washingtonpost.com/education/2020/02/15/theres-lot-talk-about-changing-college-admissions-after-varsity-blues-scandal-dont-hold-your-breath/.

Strauss, V. (2020, February 15). It looks like the beginning of the end of America's obsession with student standardized tests. *The Washington Post.* Retrieved from https://www.washingtonpost.com/education/2020/06/21/it-looks-like-beginning-end-americas-obsession-with-student-standardized-tests/.

Uetricht, M. (2014). *Strike for America: Chicago teachers against austerity.* Brooklyn, NY: Verso Trade.

Vasquez Heilig, J., Brewer, T. J., & Ojeda Pedraza, J. (2018). Examining the Myth of Accountability, High-Stakes Testing, and the Achievement Gap. *Journal of Family Strengths, 18*(1), 9.

Will, G. F. (2014, January 15). George Will: Doubts over Common Core won't be easily dismissed. *The Washington Post.* Retrieved from https://www.washingtonpost.com/opinions/george-will-doubts-over-common-core-wont-be-easily-dismissed/2014/01/15/68cecb88-7df3-11e3-93c1-0e888170b723_story.html.

Williams, J. P. (2014, February 27). *Who is fighting against Common Core? USNews.* Retrieved from https://www.usnews.com/news/special-reports/a-guide-to-common-core/articles/2014/02/27/who-is-fighting-against-common-core.

INDEX